D1579052

Psychic Art

Seeing is Believing

By Marion Voy

Voyager Publishing

Life is for living – for looking forward and finding joy

Marion x

ISBN 0-9551860-0-5
ISBN 978-0-9551860-0-4

Printed and bound in the UK by Smart Design and Print Ltd
www.smartdesignandprint.com

Photography and graphics by Davidson Read Associates.
www.davidsonread.com

Marion Voy
57 Brierbush Road
Macmerry
East Lothian
Scotland.
EH33 1PR.

www.marionvoy.com

This book is dedicated to my dad,
William Ritchie Whaley

To the soul I know as father,
whose life entwines with mine.
For as we live our lives together
we are joined for all of time.

Your love for me is faultless.
My love for you the same.
We will always be together,
No matter time or place.

For as we grow together
Our souls are heard above.
We will journey towards the father
and the joy of perfect love.

Acknowledgements

I have been very lucky in that, I have always been surrounded by people in my life who have loved me and I thank them and thank God.

My sisters Corrinne and Byrnice, my brother Ritchie, and my mum and dad Frances and Bill Whaley.

I am also thankful that my own family, my ex-husband Clive and our children Lynsey, Colin and Paul have not only loved me but have accepted me as I am, even although Lynsey still describes me as a psycho instead of a psychic!

I also would like to thank Harrison for his energy and spirit by making me look at the bigger picture, to think outside the box.

Colin D Read, without whom the book would have been impossible to collate. His firm volunteered to do all the photography work for me free of charge. Colin's philosophy is 'givers gain' so thank you Colin for all you have given me.

I would also like to thank everyone who sent me photographs of their loved ones and allowed me to include their stories in this book.

Linda, at Smart Design and Print for her professionalism and for keeping me calm.

Last, but not least, I would like to thank Gordon. Gordon I met last New Years Day.

I had dropped Harrison off at work and because the buses were not running, I offered to give his work colleague Gordon a lift home. Gordon asked what line of work I was in and when I told him he was very enthusiastic and mentioned that he had bought Gordon Smiths book as a Christmas present for his mum and was fascinated by it. Gordon had so many questions that needed answered. I dropped him off ten minutes later but within those ten minutes, I had decided that I was going to write a book of my own experiences. My goal was that by the following New Year, I would have my own book published and I would give him the first copy.

A few words from a stranger that gave me inspiration and motivation. Remember this when you next have a conversation with someone you just happen to meet by chance.

Marion

PSYCHIC ART - Seeing is believing

Contents

In the beginning was the light.
In the beginning was God.
In the beginning there was peace
harmony and understanding.
The spirit was pure, the light was bright.
We must unite to spread the light from one to another.
That one becomes two, two becomes four,
Four becomes eight and eight becomes sixteen.
That the light of the spirit once more
Shines through the density of the physical
And man can be in touch with the self.
That the emotions of darkness be diminished.
Let us teach each other to love one another.

Marion Voy

IN THE BEGINNING...

My story begins with the death of my nana, Marion Murdoch (Mainie) in November 1984. I was her first grandchild and called Marion after her. She and I were very close. I am similar in character to her in many ways; I am very organised, like to be well dressed and like to get my own way. In other words, I am a wee bit bossy!

In the autumn of 1983, she was very ill, she had a form of leukaemia and was in and out of hospital for treatment receiving blood transfusions every six weeks but she was slowly deteriorating. She and my papa, Robbie, were beginning to need more support.

One Wednesday when going to visit them I noticed the house opposite her, was up for sale. I felt that maybe it would be a great idea to buy it and move in near them. I would be close at hand if and when they needed me. Impulsively I knocked on the door and luckily, Mrs Scott was at home and showed me around the house. I immediately felt that this house was for me and I decided to buy the house before I had even seen the upstairs.

Sometimes you just know when things feel right. I liked the house. It had three large bedrooms, whereas the flat we were in the bedrooms were small, and it also had a garden and a garage. The only problem was the 'closing date ' for offers was Friday. I phoned our solicitor and he said that was not a problem he would send someone to value it on the Thursday and we could certainly have an offer in before twelve noon on the Friday.

Another small problem was that my husband, Clive who was a long distance lorry driver, was driving somewhere in England and was not due home until Friday. I could not get in touch with him! That was the days before mobile phones! I decided to 'go for it 'anyway, as I said I'm a wee bit bossy.

I put an offer in and bought the house without consulting him. On Friday when Clive did come home, I knew I was going to have to confess to what I had done, so I told him I had bought him a present- a garage. He looked confused "where am I going to put it, we live in an upstairs flat?"I told him not to worry about it, that there was a house attached to the garage! Thankfully, he liked the house, and we were set to move three months later on 1 December.

The first of December I had the keys for the new house in my pocket and I am standing at the graveside watching my nanas coffin being lowered into the ground. I feel so sad and disappointed but so angry," why did you have to die? I am moving in across from you and you are not there, why?

I heard her voice in my head say, "Marion you'll be okay you need to move anyway - you are pregnant ".

I immediately started to argue with her that I couldn't be, I had a coil fitted and anyway my son Colin was only eight months old, I couldn't be!!

At the time the conversation seemed natural to me but later that night I did think it was a bit strange and wanted to disbelieve it - there was no way that I could be pregnant.

I was, and my youngest son Paul was born the following July. In Scotland we have a saying than when one life ends another begins and I have found this to be true in many instances. I missed my nana so much but I felt her presence around me often and drew comfort from that. When I say I felt her presence, what I could feel was a sense of feeling, the glow you get when someone loves you and I could smell Kiku, a perfume that was her favourite, and every so often, I could hear her voice in my head talking to me.

My papa never really got over her death. He would sit for hours never saying a word. He missed her so much. He too had his own questions.

Where will I go when my time is done?
Where will I rest my head?
Where will be the one I love?
Who took the step ahead?
Will she be waiting proud and erect?
Will she be smiling and looking ahead?
Does she know that I have waited so long?
To be by her side where I belong
Oh for the joy of the days gone by,
To be relived and captured once more.
For our youth and our laughter mingled again
With the love and the light in her eyes.
My dear I am waiting, it seems so long
But one day it will be no more
For we will be united in God's holy love
And our life eternal will reign.

My papa joined her in the spirit world three months later. He took a heart attack and died, although my mum would say he died not from the heart attack but from a broken heart. When you have lived as a couple for over forty years and then your partner dies, it must be as if a part of you has died. How do you begin to adjust?

The week after his death, I was almost asleep in bed when I was aware that he was peeking his head round my bedroom door. I smiled and felt myself float off the bed and move to where he was and I embraced him. It was a wonderful experience of connecting on a completely different emotion of love. It was like a lifetime of love we had for each other contained in that moment, and I remember thinking "well that'll frighten the life out of him!" mainly because he was not a demonstrative man and rarely showed affection but I knew it was his way of loving me, saying goodbye and letting me know he was contented to be with my nana. Then I floated back to were my body was, back to the bed. I felt an amazing sense of peace. I felt I had received love in every particle of my being and fell into a peaceful yet deep sleep. That experience certainly made me think.

I was not shocked by the fact that I had embraced him. I thought he would have been the one that was shocked.

How had I managed to leave my body in the bed, float to where he was, and embrace him?

What part of me embraced him when my physical body was still lying on the bed?

Is that what it feels like when we die, we just leave our body behind and the thinking, feeling part of ourselves moves on, but moves on to where?

Where was he living, what was he doing and who else was he with?

That feeling of love was so pure. Why had I had never really experienced it in my material life? I was fortunate in that I was surrounded by people who loved me but I had never felt love like that before.

Was that a spiritual love that perhaps we do not allow ourselves to experience in the material world because we are afraid to open our hearts completely and love unconditionally?

If that quality of love could be experienced how could I create that in my life?

So many questions that I needed answers for. I started to talk to them both in my head. I felt that maybe they would know the answers. I also started to chat to my nana about everyday things, the same way I would if she were still living. My nana would often tell me things that were going to happen within the family and would visit me in my dreams.

She told me that my sister Byrnice was going to have a baby, which I must say I found hard to believe considering that Byrnice and her husband Robin were separated, but I thought I would wait and see. She certainly had been correct when she told me that I was pregnant.

I missed her so much and wanted to know more –

Where was she?

Were they together?

How was I able to speak to her sometimes but not all the time?

Where did God fit into this?

What was the meaning of life?

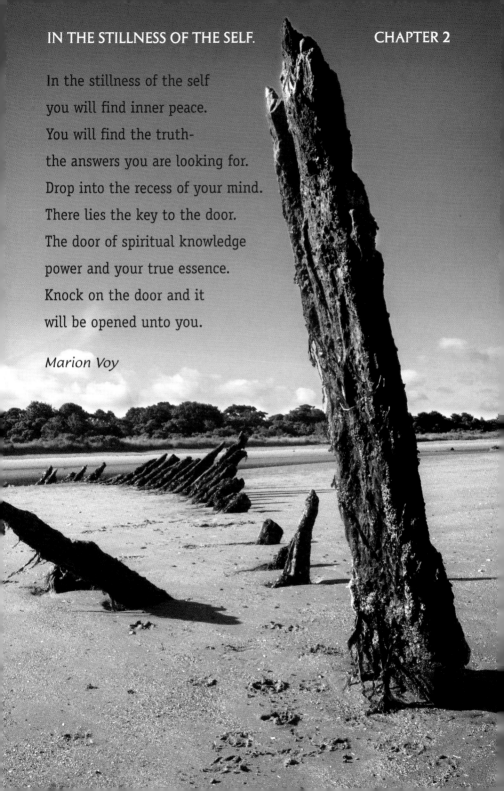

In the stillness of the self
you will find inner peace.
You will find the truth-
the answers you are looking for.
Drop into the recess of your mind.
There lies the key to the door.
The door of spiritual knowledge
power and your true essence.
Knock on the door and it
will be opened unto you.

Marion Voy

I was desperate to find out more but did not know where to go to get the answers.

In January, at my nephew Craig's christening I was very emotional and uplifted in the church and knew what I was seeking was spiritual but I felt that for me, something was missing within the Orthodox Church. I could feel the warmth, comfort and love within the church but knew I was seeking more and would need to keep looking.

I had this overwhelming drive to find the answers to my questions. I mentioned this to my mum who confessed that the previous week she had gone to Portobello Spiritualist Church run by Bernice Winstanly and her husband Jack, so I decided to go along and I immediately felt at home.

Spiritualist Churches are different from orthodox churches in that each week they will have a visiting medium. A medium being·a person who gives messages from people in the spirit world to people who are in the material world. The medium acts as a messenger.

The service consists of:

The chairperson welcoming the congregation, to ensure that each person feels relaxed.

OPENING HYMN. The singing helps everyone to get rid of any tension or worry they may have brought with him or her into the church. As you sing you need to breath in and as you sing out you release that energy. Singing also unites everyone. I believe that we each have our own individual voice vibration and as you sing then those in the spirit world hear you. Almost like an individual ring tone (for those of you who have mobile phones) waiting to be answered.

OPENING PRAYER. The purpose of the opening prayer is that as you close your eyes you close out the material world and connect with your heart chakra - you open your heart to your spiritual self and to a higher source.

READING OF THE HEALING LIST. The list is made up of people who are in need of healing and upliftment and each member sends love from the heart to these names - absent healing.

READING - A reading is given by a different member of the congregation each week. The reading chosen can be anything that the person thinks will be spiritually enlightening to the congregation and readings can be taken from the Bible, the Koran, Buddhist teachings, poetry, and philosophy. The understanding within the church being that we are all on the path seeking spiritual enlightenment and should be open to all teachings and embrace all cultures and religions. We should be tolerant of each other's views and that we each are responsible for finding the truth. Finding God within ourselves. I think that is what I like about the church - you are not told what you should believe. You are encouraged to search for enlightenment, encouraged to meditate and find within yourself a sense of God,'at-oneness' and peace.

ADDRESS. After the reading, the visiting medium will give an inspired address on that reading. By inspired address - what I mean is that the visiting medium will tune in to his or her guides and will speak words of wisdom that relate to the reading. Years later, when I first started to take church services I found this very daunting. It is not as if you can prepare for it, as you do not know what the reading will be about. You have to put your trust in your guides that when you stand up to speak, the wisdom will flow and make sense!

HYMN. The purpose of this hymn is to create energy and to allow the medium to prepare him/herself to tune in and give messages from people in the spirit world.

MESSAGES. Communication from the medium to people in the congregation.

CLOSING HYMN. The purpose of which is to allow everyone to close - you opened in the opening hymn so you close or ground your energy with the closing hymn.

At the end of the service, there is a sense of peace, wellbeing and upliftment.

After a short interval then those that wish can receive spiritual healing.

At that time in Britain alternative healing was almost non-existent, e.g., no one practised Reiki, Sekem or other energy work, and so I was fascinated by the results that were being achieved through spiritual healing.

Mum, dad and I joined the development circle in the church that was run by Jack Winstanley, a truly gentle and spiritual man who was a healer within the church. We were in his circle for many years and experimented with physical mediumship as well as mental mediumship.

It was at this time Channel Four put on a program hosted by Tobias Churton called 'The Gnostics 'and when I heard the opening lines 'THESE ARE THE SECRET SAYINGS THAT THE LIVING JESUS SPOKE...'

Those words struck a chord in my heart and I just knew that this was what I was looking for.

The program looked at the scrolls which were discovered buried under sand in December 1945 in Quasr, a village 6 kilometres from Nag Hammadi by three brothers, Muhammad, Khalif and Abu-al-Majd. The documents thought to have been written 120 -150AD were written in Coptic (an ancient Egyptian language written in Greek letters - the language of the New Testament) and comprised of 'Gospel of Thomas ', Aprocrylon of James ', Gospel of Truth, and many gospels that are not included in the bible.

When a blind man and one who sees are in darkness, they are no different from one another, when the light comes then he who sees will. (Gospel of Philip).

My understanding of the Gnostics was that they believed that we each have a personal spiritual relationship with God, we do not need a priest, minister or medium to communicate on our behalf. That if we sit quiet and are in touch with our spiritual self then we will hear the answers to our question, the truth will be made known to us.

'Seek and yea shall find'

'Ask and it will be given unto you

I started to meditate and found that I was being given the answers to my questions. At first I worried that it was my 'imagination' but as I got used to entering that altered state I found I was going deeper and deeper almost like a sleep state and it would be difficult to remember what I had heard. I always kept a pen and paper at my side and as I received the information, I would quickly write it down, something I always advise others to do.

I found that it could not have been my imagination for various reasons. Sometimes I couldn't fully understand the philosophy and very often disagreed with it, but this was part of my learning, my searching for truth and I found that what I may have not understood or agreed with, on reading what I had written six months later, it had become clear and I had accepted it as truth. Interestingly enough I found my handwriting when meditating was very different from my normal handwriting and later found out that it would vary with different guides.

I asked for guiding energy to come forward and help me on my journey and this energy I recognised as a male figure in white hooded robes that I named 'Pilgrim'. He told me the following:-

11

"In the stillness of the self you will find inner peace. You will find the truth, the answers that you are looking for. Drop into the recess of your mind. There lies the key to the door. The door of spiritual knowledge, power and your true essence. Knock on the door and it will be opened unto you. We are ready to welcome you to our realms. The realms of angelic wisdom, truth and being. Lighten the load you are carrying. Allow the baggage to fall away. Lighten the physical essence, the pull from the material body and you will be able to travel within the realms. We wait to beckon you to the work ahead that is to be done on the material. Do not worry; the pressure you feel from the physical is normal. You must break the chord that ties you to the earth plane to be truly free and to become amongst us. It has to be done and has needed to be done for some time. Only you can do this. Shed the thoughts that keep you to the earth plane. Never mind the thoughts of others, you are pure and true, do not take on their negative thought patterns".

In other words, the key to the door is meditation.

Through meditation, you can know yourself on many levels and in that knowing understand who you are. Meditation teaches you to go into the silence and within that silence recognise that you are a part of all living things in this world and the next. It teaches control of the mind and emotions and is a healing or a balancing of the energy you carry within your auric field. It also allows communicating on a higher level.

If you are searching for your own truth know that the answers lie deep within you. In meditation, you have access to your higher self, access to all the lives you have ever lived and therefore access to all the knowledge you have ever learned.

You have access to guides and guardian angels and all the knowledge and wisdom that they can give to you.

MEDITATION

Preparation.

1. Choose a time when you will not be disturbed.
2. Turn of the phone / doorbell.
3. If others are in the house tell them you are meditating and do not want to be disturbed.
4. Wear loose clothing.
5. Pick a time when you are alert. If you are tired or have just eaten then wait until later.
6. Choose suitable music and do not have it too loud.

To Start.

1. Sit comfortably.
2. Close your eyes, take a deep breath, and as you release that breath – let go – let go any tension or worry.
3. Take your attention to your heart and feel the emotion of love within.
4. Now concentrate on sending that love around your body, so that you are surrounded in pink light.
5. Ask or pray for what you want, whether it be answers to questions, help or healing for someone you are concerned about.

If you have a question, write it down, meditate and whilst still in that state listen for the answers. If you do not hear, ask for the answers to be shown to you. You will find that by coincidence, someone or something will point you in the right direction, you may be given a book that has the answer or it may even be shown to you in a dream.

The only problem I had was that having opened that door I was being wakened in the middle of the night with information. I kept a notebook at the side of my bed and would quickly write what was being given. At first I was excited about this but having three young children to look after I found I became tired and crabby if I did not get enough sleep. So I decided to make a deal. I would meditate every morning at 10 o'clock and any information to be given was to be given then and only then.

When I look back, this practise increased my knowledge of spiritual matters and taught me to be still - to relax my energy physically and emotionally so that my spiritual energy was more dominant. This in turn makes me aware of my spiritual senses of seeing hearing and feeling. By that I mean clairvoyance, clairaudience and clairsentience. These senses I was able to use later on when 'giving messages' from people in the spirit world, but at that time I was only concerned with my spiritual journey and understanding myself.

I had an ally in my dad who was also on a quest to know the truth and we would spend hours discussing different religions and their understanding or way to God. He used to joke that between us we had all the answers *"If I don't know the answer our Marion will"*. I wish that were true - the more I learned the more I realised there was to learn, but I was enjoying the journey and still am.

I came to realise that spiritual wisdom was not about mental knowledge, it is wisdom of the heart, an emotion, and an inner state of being that is accessible to us all.

If you are searching for your own answers, searching for that sense of inner peace and contentment then I would strongly recommend that you take some time each day to meditate. To connect with yourself, to love and accept yourself. You will be surprised at how quickly you can rid yourself of depression, illness, stress and feel more confident and happy.

One of us is missing.

Has bolted from the fold.

Gone to join another flock

of which you have been told.

Gone to join the father,

and help him with his work.

To join all flocks together.

That man may live in love.

To be at peace as brothers,

as upon this earth we dwell.

Learning from each other

and knowing all too well.

That one day we all will make

the journey, to join the flock above.

And meet with those we miss so much

And whom we truly love.

Marion Voy

On the 9th of June 1986, my brother Ritchie was killed. It was a beautiful Sunday morning and our quiet village of Port Seton had an aura of peace around it. It had been the gala day the day before and that sense of togetherness and celebration was in the air, the streets still decked with flags.

My brother had left early on his motorbike, a Suzuki 1300 GSXR, his pride and joy, to take his girlfriend Margaret to North Berwick for work, before heading back to Port Seton to meet up with his friends from the bike club. He dropped Margaret off and was driving back up the coast road when he was involved in an accident and killed instantly.

That morning my dad had a dream in which my papa was with him. They were at a funeral and my papa was saying, "that was a good turnout ", at which my dad was so shocked he woke up. He had a bad feeling in the pit of his stomach, he just knew that something was terribly wrong and on finding that my mum was not in the house he phoned me to see if she was with me.

She was not - she had wakened early, had a premonition that something was wrong with Ritchie, and had actually driven down to North Berwick to look for him. Whilst she was gone, the police arrived to break the bad news to my dad that a lad had been killed on a motorbike, which was licensed in Ritchie's name. The police wanted someone to come to identify the body.

My sister Byrnice and I went because my dad wanted to wait for my mum to return, to break to her the tragic news.

Dad was left in the house waiting for Mum and because he did not know what to do, he started to vacuum the kitchen. As he was vacuuming, the motor died down slowly and as he walked over to have a look at the switch, it started up again. This continued another twice until dad asked "Is that you Ritchie?" and it stopped.

My sister Byrnice and I went to the Mortuary to identify Ritchie. That was a weird experience. When we saw Ritchie, I was shocked that the energy that was Ritchie was not there. All that was there, was a hard almost china shell that we recognised as his body. I had this overwhelming urge to sing which at the time seemed ridiculous. I needed to do that and we asked the police officer if he would leave us for a few moments and Byrnice and I sang the hymn 'Nearer my God To Thee '.I felt strong and comforted by doing that and I could feel Ritchie's presence standing watching over us.

The next few days it was as if time had stopped. We were so shocked at loosing Ritchie. We did a lot of talking and a lot of soul searching - each of us having our own different psychic experiences of Ritchie's presence.

17

On the night on which he was killed I went to give my mum a cuddle before going home and all of a sudden it was as if I wasn't really there. I was aware of being Ritchie - tall, strong, masculine and as I looked down I could see the big bikers boots and I could hear his voice in my head saying 'mum it's me '. I felt totally spaced out, there but not there. It was as if I was standing behind my own body and there was this strong electric field around us both. This was the first time I had felt spirit coming in so close within my auric field. I felt elated and it prepared me for it happening in the future when spirit wanted to communicate through me with their family.

The day after he was killed my daughter Lynsey who was only four ran through to my bedroom in the morning very excited and said "Mum you'll never guess what I seen in my 'window 'last night". Her window was how she described her third eye, the images she saw.

"I saw nana and papa and the band were playing and Uncle Ritchie was there too. Why was he there? "

A question that I too needed the answer too, why had he died?

Lynsey said that he was with my nana and papa and that the band was playing. Was this some kind of welcome into the spirit world?

My daughter from an early age was very intuitive as are all children, and I explained as best as I could that he had had an accident on his motorbike and had gone to heaven.

That day mum and dad came up to my house to spend some time with the kids bringing with them my brothers wee dog Pip, a Jack Russell terrier. Mum said it was almost as if the dog knew Ritchie was not coming back because Pip always slept on Ritchie's bed even when he was away for a few days but last night she had slept on their bed. When it became time for them to go home, Pip hid in my house and would not go with them and so I acquired a lodger. On looking back, I think this was an omen because mum and dad moved in with me eighteen months later. They too found it difficult to fill the void that had been left by Ritchie's death. He was the only son, the youngest and my mum's favourite.

The next week the house was filled with psychic activity -, tumble dryer and kettle would go on when no-one was near and whenever Ritchie's girlfriend's name -"Margaret" was mentioned the lights would dim and then lighten up again. Which was strange because we did not have a dimmer switch. He was desperately trying to comfort us and let us know that he lived on.

Having spoken to many people over the years who have been bereaved, they too tell of strange things happening very similar to what we were experiencing, visions, dreams, hearing footsteps, electrical activity etc, and I do think that our loved ones are trying to comfort us and let us know that their soul lives on and to give us strength to help us to move forward through the sense of loss and grief that we are experiencing.

It strikes me as strange that we all will experience grief at some point in our lives yet our culture does not seem to prepare us for that, resulting in many people taking years to come to terms with bereavement and some people never managing to reach that space.

I can only imagine the pain that my parents were experiencing following Ritchie's death. I had lost my only brother, but the pain of loosing a son has to be so much more. As a family we all felt so lost and fragile, each of us trying to be strong, not for ourselves but for each other.

Mum and dad were booked to go on holiday the following Saturday to the Arthur Findlay College in Stanstead to do a course they were interested in that related to psychic development.

At first mum wanted to cancel but we all said no that they should go. I am a great believer that everything happens for a reason and that there must be a reason for them to be there. I felt that the week there would be healing for them both.

If they were going to get help then that was the place to be. The college runs various courses on spiritualism, healing, awareness and spiritual development. The college was left to the Spiritualist movement by Arthur Findlay and it is a beautiful peaceful retreat in the country, cut off from the outside world as there is no television, newspapers and phones are limited. They decided that they would go and while they were there, they received wonderful messages from both Gordon Higginson and Ruby Grey. I thank God that they had booked to go there at a time when they needed so much. I do not think it was a coincidence. They were there because that is where they were meant to be.

Whilst they were there, Coral Polge a well-known psychic artist was also there. Coral Polge tuned in to the spirit world and was able to draw portraits of people who had passed to the spirit world. Unfortunately, mum did not receive a drawing from her. My mum felt that at that time she was so raw with grief that she would have given anything for a spiritual portrait of Ritchie, she was so desperate. She vowed that no matter how long it took, she was going to work in that way; she was going to draw spiritual portraits to help people who were grieving. In our circle she voiced her commitment and asked for guides to help her. I must admit I was surprised mainly due to the fact that mum is not an artist and cannot draw!, but I was not going to discourage her. I had already decided that I wanted to work for spirit giving messages to people who were bereaved. I listened to the taped message that Gordon Higginson and Ruby Grey had given to my parents. Messages that really uplifted and helped all the family.

The first Father's Day after Ritchie's death, I was meditating and thinking how difficult this day would be for my dad when I was aware of Ritchie's voice giving me a poem to give to my dad.

> *To the soul I know as father,*
> *Whose life entwines with mine.*
> *For as we live our lives together*
> *We are joined for all of time.*
>
> *Your love for me is faultless.*
> *My love for you the same.*
> *We will always be together,*
> *No matter time or place.*
>
> *For as we grow together*
> *Our souls are heard above.*
> *We will journey towards the father*
> *And the joy of perfect love.*

When I gave dad the poem he read it and cried, we all did but it brought a sense of upliftment and hope.

Ritchie's death as you can imagine had a huge impact on all the family. It brought a change of direction in my own spiritual quest. I had been interested in spiritual philosophy but now I was determined that I was going to be able to receive spirit communication and pass it on to people who were bereaved. People who were going through that awful sense of loss and confusion that we were feeling, in the hope that they would be able to get some comfort from the communication, and that they would realise that there is life after death and start to look within themselves and connect to their own spirit and find a sense of peace.

The pain of bereavement is like no other pain. It hits you in the pit of your stomach and you feel like you are in a never-ending nightmare, somewhere far from reality. Some days you wake up in the morning and for a moment, you feel normal and then you remember and the grief comes in like a tidal wave to hit you and you feel you are drowning.

Hope comes in snatches, dreams in which you can hear their voice saying "I am okay", only to waken up too soon and the moment is lost but the yearning to be with them just one more time is intense.

Days when you feel you cannot get out of bed but have to. There are some days when you do feel that bit stronger but have to give that strength to other family members who are having a bad day. Tired and exhausted, yet not being able to sleep but when you do it is a wonderful escape from reality.

The trivial things that people worry about has no consequence, everything takes on a different perspective. You no longer care how you look, if you have money or if the washing machine blows up. You just do not have the energy to worry over such things.

You are not afraid to die anymore. In fact, you might even welcome it, just to know the truth. Is there life after death? At least you would know. It would not just be hope. The hope that you would be reunited. Yet for that to happen you would need to leave behind the rest of your loved ones. What would be better?

You care only about your family, the ones left here and about strengthening these relationships. Yet the weird thing is – you feel alone, very solitary, almost afraid to love them too much because how could you bear to loose them? Yet you have the need to love them so very very much, so that if anything did happen then you would have no regrets and maybe, just maybe that would make it easier.

Grief can be a very solitary process in that the tendency is to withdraw from those we love and go deep within ourselves. Perhaps because we have no energy, physically, mentally or emotionally to give to others. Grief has a similar energy to depression.

In many cases especially where a child has been lost, very often the parents will separate or even divorce. This is partly because they cannot deal with the other person's grief as well as their own and because grief is a very individual thing. We each deal with grief in different ways and one partner may not understand the other partner's way of dealing with their grief. Some people have the need to talk and remember, others want to block out the pain and try to forget sometimes though excessive work, drink and even drugs.

I have found that I have grieved in different ways, or the level of grief has been different for the people I have grieved for. This has been determined by the relationship between us, the circumstances surrounding their death and my own spiritual understanding of death and its meaning at that time.

I made a commitment to my guides that I would spend the time it required to develop mediumship to help others as I had been helped, by mediums such as Ruby Grey, Bernice Winstanly, Gordon Higginson and many others.

We had many questions.

Why had Ritchie died so young?

Is it the case that when you have served some kind of purpose on earth you leave?

Is there an afterlife ?

Where do they live that life?

Is there a heaven, a hell or different levels of existence?

Do you look back on your life and are you held accountable for the good or bad deeds you have done?

Do you reincarnate?

If so, how soon?

My nana's message to me came true in that my sister Byrnice did have a baby. On the 23rd of March, nine months after Ritchie's death, my sister gave birth to a wee boy and named him Richard. Once again as one soul left our lives for the spirit world, another soul was born into our lives on the material. My mum has six grandsons, yet Richard, or Dickie as we affectionately call him is the only one who has an interest in motorbikes.

I still was not getting all the answers I needed and found that I was drawing to me like-minded people who were also searching. I decided to start a meditation circle in my house. Within that circle we asked the questions and our guides came forward giving us the philosophy we craved for. It was a good circle consisting of mum, dad, my sister Byrnice and friends Brian Webb, Walter Davidson and John Macleod. John's guides always gave philosophy in poetry, which he later had published. Quiet Flows the Love, a lovely book of upliftment and inspiration.

One night before our meditation circle, we had been debating reincarnation. Was it possible that this could happen or was it just a figment of the imagination?

During the meditation, I was reliving a scene from a Native American Indian Village. I was an Indian female and was talking with a male that I recognised as my brother Ritchie. There seemed to be a sense of sadness, fear and helplessness around us. Then I was aware of the smell of smoke. I was terrified and confused. The village was being burned down by our enemies another Indian tribe and I could hear the children screaming, they were trapped in the burning tents. I was choking from the smoke. There was nothing but chaos. Part of this scene I had seen many times before as nightmares from early childhood and that was the reason why I was a bit neurotic about fire and slept with a hammer under my bed, so that if there ever was a fire in my house my children would not be trapped. As with the nightmare it was so awful I came out of the meditation quickly but I recognised that my fear of fire had nothing to do with this lifetime, it was a past memory. A fear I had carried from one lifetime to another. I also recognised why I had needed to sing when I had gone to identify my brother's dead body. That too was part of a memory, a custom lying dormant in my subconscious mind carried from one lifetime to another.

My sister Byrnice was also aware of seeing an Indian lifetime that we all seemed to share but what was most surprising was my mum and dads vision in the meditation.

Mum had seen herself as a young slim Indian girl who having hidden her elderly father in the bushes by the river was being pursued by an Indian on a horse. The Indian caught her raped her and killed her by putting his hands round her throat and strangling her.

The Indian on the horse was my dad.

Dad had seen the same scene and was very shocked. We all were when they told us what they had seen. My mum and dad were very close. Could it be possible that in another life, they were enemies and he had killed her? The funny thing was, mum in this life would not let anyone put his or her hands on her throat.

That night certainly gave us plenty to think about.

Had we all lived together in a previous lifetime?

Why were we together this lifetime?

Did we all carry fears from one lifetime to the next?

If this was true of our family- were all families the same? Is there a reason that they are together in this lifetime?

If we had lived together in the past, and the present, did that mean we would share lives together in the future?

23

I try to portray who I am
The way I wish to be remembered.
I want to be remembered
Not for the pain nor the sadness
That has been left behind.
I want to portray who I am
For the love and the memories we share.
I need to portray that love is eternal
And we will meet again someday.
I'd like to portray that I'm around
Perhaps when you least expect.
I wish to portray that I love you still
And that I always will.

Marion Voy

The next few years were busy - Ritchie's death had created a void in the house, a void my mum and dad found hard to cope with and they eventually moved in with Clive and I. Looking back I was so glad that we had moved to the larger house, a house we were able to extend to accommodate us all. The reason I had bought the house was to give support to my grandparents but that was not to be. Instead, we were giving support to my parents.

I was raising my three young children, working full-time attending church, sitting in circle, meditating and coming to terms with the loss of my brother. I had also started giving short 'messages ' to people in the church and I was going to other churches with my friend Val Robson to take the church service. Oh how I wish I had the energy I had back then.

Every Sunday we would travel to different churches in Scotland. Falkirk, Kirkcaldy, Glenrothes, Perth, Broxburn, Glasgow, Bathgate, Edinburgh... and each week I would learn something more.

I have always been very analytical about my mediumship and if I felt I had not worked to the best of my ability I would come home and next day I would meditate and ask my guides "What did I do wrong?" and I would be given the answers. I found that I needed to understand how my energy field or auric field operated. I needed to be able to control it, to switch it on and off when I needed to. I needed to understand mediumship and how I was picking up the information. Sometimes I was seeing or hearing things but most of the time I was sensing the spirit person and the message that they wanted to put across. I made many mistakes but I learned from them and if you are trying to develop mediumship I would say to you not to be afraid to get it wrong, learn from it - that is experience. Often I would get it wrong because I would try to translate what I was seeing rather than just saying what I seen even though it perhaps did not make sense to me.

My dad was even more analytical than I was. He was able to give wonderful philosophy but always doubted his ability. He worried that it was his thoughts and not those of his guides. So much so that one time I taped him speaking so that he would realise that even the phrasing of the words and the way they were said, was very different to how he spoke. My dad was an uneducated man from Bellshill near Glasgow.

One Sunday nearly two years later, we were going to work in a church in Kirkcaldy and mum announced she was going to work with us and do 'spiritual drawings'. Mum had never done them before and I was shocked and worried because I was not sure how it would work and asked her what she was going to draw with? She said she did not know and took black paper and chalk that my daughter Lynsey had been drawing on! She had the determination and confidence that she would be able to do it.

The first spirit that came through was a gentleman named James who had died from a heart attack and he had came through to reassure his wife that he was alright, and had met up with her mother whom he had been close to. They both wanted her to take care of her health, which had deteriorated since the passing of her husband in August that year. The drawing was the woman's husband. She was delighted, her face lit up and you could see a peace come over her. Although she had had messages from her husband before, she needed something more. The drawing was the proof she was seeking.

This was what mum had been waiting for and praying for - a chance to help uplift someone who was bereaved, to help that person take that first step forward after the devastation of loosing someone that was loved so much and whose death left a huge space in her life.

'Ask and you will receive ' Mum had certainly asked to be an instrument to help others in this way and through meditation, patience, and dedication it had finally been given. She had knocked on the door and it had been opened.

There was still a lot to learn and we found that perhaps because we were so close and were meditating together, we were able to work together. If I was giving a message, then mum was able to also link in and draw either the person in the spirit world that I was communicating with or another family member. That was the beginning of mum's work. At that time mum drew on black paper with white chalk. The drawings were basic, firstly because she is not a trained artist and secondly, the drawing had to be drawn in the time I took to pass on the message. Sometimes within as little as eight minutes, yet they were good enough to be recognised. We have noticed that often the person will come forward in the drawing when they were slightly younger than when they died, especially if they had been ill for a long time. It is as if they want to be remembered when they looked their best and not at a time of sadness for the family. Very occasionally mum has drawn pictures of people who are still living, the reason being that the person in the spirit world is sending them healing because they are ill or are going through an emotionally difficult period.

Over the years the drawings have changed, mum now draws on white paper with black pencil and the drawings have improved as her connection with spirit has become stronger. I am still amazed that she can tune in to spirit and draw a portrait all within ten minutes.

We both enjoy working for spirit and working with each other. We seem to be able to link well together, maybe because we are mother and daughter, maybe because we spent years meditating together in our circle.

I have been given permission from people who have received messages, to include their messages and portraits in this book. I asked them to send me photos of the person in the portrait. Although the photos may have been taken at a different age from the spirit portrait, you can still see the resemblance. The early drawings you can see are on black paper. You can also see the change in the drawings as mum's connection became stronger. I have included these early drawings, mainly to let you see that if you are developing any type of mediumship your ability will improve with time and dedication.

 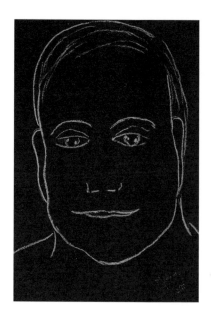

This first drawing was drawn for Elizabeth Anderson and was of her grandfather. The drawing was done not long after Elizabeth's father had died and both she and her mum Betty were finding it very difficult to cope. They found it comforting to know that both her dad and grandfather were together.

As you can see, the drawing is basic but the resemblance is still there.

If you are trying to develop this or any type of mediumship then remember like everything else in life you need to start at the beginning. All too often we expect instant results and get frustrated if that is not so.

The second drawing was for Mary Ellen Barton. The message was from her mum and was concerning Mary Ellen's daughter Terry who was going through a very difficult time in her life. Terry who has three young children was in the process of separating from her husband and Mary Ellen was naturally worried about her. More so, because Terry was living in America whilst Mary Ellen was in Scotland. The message was to reassure Mary Ellen that Terry would get through this stormy period in her life and would be able to move on.

The drawing was of Terry.

Psychic Art - Case Study

Marion wanted to speak to me and said she had a young laddie in the spirit world who was about seventeen years old and that he had died tragically in suspicious circumstances. She stated that there were four other people there at the time and that one of the lads had what looked like a tattoo of a spider on his hand. I was stunned. The young boy was my sister's son Kevin. Marion said he was sending his love and support to his mum and that I was to tell her that justice would be done. At that time the case into his death was being heard in court and my sister was having a hard time listening to what had happened. Justice was done and the person found responsible was sentenced to seven years in jail.

She said Kevin was with Bobby, John and Alex and that he was talking about football and waving a Hearts scarf.

Bobby is my grandfather, and John and Alex are Kevin's uncles. John at one time was the manager of Hearts.

Marion then said that he had with him a young girl in the spirit world that belonged to me but that she had died as a baby and also that she looked liked someone I knew. I had lost a baby and I had been thinking of her a lot lately because of my sister loosing her son and I had wondered what she would have looked like had she lived. The drawing was of a young girl who actually resembles my niece Sharon who is a few years older than my daughter would have been. So the drawing that has helped answer a question I had about her.

Thankyou, *Gail*.

Psychic Art - Case Study

Marion said she had a man in the spirit world whose name was Robert. That he had a link to my dad and that they were very close. She described Robert as very frail before he died and that he always wore a hat and a maroon scarf, and that he liked to whistle and would play tricks with his hat.

Marion said he was sending love to my mum and that she needed a plate of home-made soup. She also said he was with his dad, Harry who had been a coal miner. The last thing she said was "Have you found what is in the book?"

I was so pleased to get the drawing because I had been saying to my mum that it was a shame that we did not have a photograph of my uncle Robert who was my dad's cousin. They were very close, they would go down to the Legion for a drink and when they came home my uncle Robert would tease us kids by playing a tin whistle and we would hide his hat from him. While they were at the Legion mum would make soup for them coming home to try to sober them up. Harry is my grandad and he worked in the pits.

I was not too sure what the last part of the message meant, until two months later. My cousin was looking for directions in the A.A. book and out dropped the photo you see of my uncle Robert.

Many thanks for the message and the drawing, *G.Nevison.*

Psychic Art - Case Study

 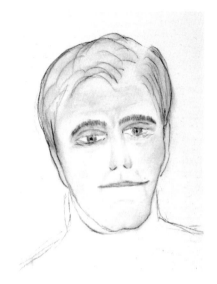

I lost my dad in December 2003, so it was comforting to know that he was with his brother, who died ten months previously. You started by saying my dad wanted to move and reorganise everything and that you thought this was symbolic and related to my own life at this time. You described my dad as quiet but stubborn, which is correct. You spoke about fluid, that you felt it had to do with the knee. Both my dad and I have had problems with fluid but not on the knee.

You said that I have to write things down. I hope this will help as I have a lot of turmoil within, screaming to get out. Something my dad brought through was that I have to have confidence within myself and to move on and do something. That I find very hard since I have very low self-esteem. But I am trying.

What enlightened me was the fact that you mentioned my uncle who was a heavy smoker and the banter that was surrounding you, between my dad and uncle. Like you said , they were like chalk and cheese but the rapport between them was something else.

You also mentioned a woman next to them – small rotund by a name that sounded like Margaret. The description is of my grandmother whose name was Marjory.

The drawing is of my dad and I was so pleased as I am putting together a scrap book of his life at the moment.

Many thanks, *Carole Mitchell*.

Psychic Art - Case Study

Dear Marion,

I had a reading done by you at the fund raiser for the pipe band in Prestonpan's Labour Club in March.

You picked me out of the audience and said that my mother was speaking to you from the spirit world and that she had wanted to connect with someone whose name began with M. My name is Mary. She was concerned because I was unwell and there was a lot of stress within the family. That was true I have been unwell recently and the last two years have been very stressful due to family problems. My Uncle James, Uncle Tom and Uncle Sandy came through and wanted remembered to my brother James. I do not have a good memory but that is what I remember of the reading. The picture was my mum when she was younger and I have enclosed a photo.

Yours sincerely,

Mary Redpath.

Psychic Art - Case Study

My name is Janette Finnie I was one of three lucky ones that got a message you don't know how good I have felt since.

You asked me to write to you as after the reading you can't always remember what you have said. Well here is what you told me.

You asked if I could relate to a dark haired women and that I looked like her. I said I could. You told me she no longer suffered, she was pain free round the chest and stomach and she was up and walking and also her throat was okay. The swelling was away from her legs and she no longer lay in bed. She had concerns for me with pain round the chest but was glad to see I was okay now and had slowed down. She was not too happy that I was in a place she did not frequent - a pub. She then brought a man forward who you described as stocky/plump build with bald head but hair round the edges. You could not pick up the name but it ended -----ie. Could I relate to this, yes I could. You said he was a recent passing but you were seeing him younger with a collar and tie. You also asked if he was a manager. He wanted me to know everything done was fine, and that where he was put was where he wanted to be. He also was free of pain now. Then back came the woman with a message from a slim man and that he sent us all his love but was busy making the soup and that he and the other man have the same name.

Then it was back to the woman but she was interrupted by another woman with back and head pains wanting to send a message to a wee girl that she was watching over and was very proud of her. Also for her to tell the other wee girl her nose is fine and it is not asthma she is a lovely wee girl. Then we went back to the first dark haired woman who said one of the family were celebrating this year it would be a small gathering but nice. Does she always refer to oor before a name as she is referring to the man as oor -----ie. She has concerns for a sister, not one of my sisters. Did she have sisters?, as this woman had a tightness of the chest and she was concerned. There was two things you said I could not relate to and they were she said. Lizzie is fine and asking for us and a connection with Glasgow.

The darked hair woman was my mum. I was only seven when she died with womb cancer and she could not digest her food properly which caused swelling of the legs and was bed ridden for 2 years before she died. The stocky/plump man she brought forward was my brother and yes his name ended in ie he was called Charlie and he was a recent death. He died last June after being diagnosed with liver cancer. The man making the soup was my Dad and yes you were right his name was the same as my brothers.

My older sister is celebrating her Ruby Wedding this year and it is only small party. I have also found out the woman called Lizzie was my Mum's best pal and my Dad had distant relations who stayed in Glasgow. The collar and tie part relating to my brother was because he was a salesman and always wore a collar and tie. We are all glad he is happy with what was done and where he was put as he was someone who enjoyed life with a new wife, so it was difficult when he passed away. I remember my Dad always making soup. Now for the other woman with back and head pains is my mother in law who was killed by a drunk driver I was with her. The little girl she is proud of is my daughter Audrey who was seven when it happened but a real Gran's girl and it is her daughter with the mark on the nose and yes she was told she had asthma but after taking inhalers for a year they said she was wrongly diagnosed.

Yours faithfully, *Janette Finney.*

Psychic Art - Case Study

Marion,

The message was from my mum and I was so pleased she came through. She died thirteen years ago and although I have gone to things like this she never comes through. You described her as a strong personality, small but a quick speaker and quite bossy at times. You also mentioned that on a Sunday she always baked, especially apple pie and that the family met at her house. That was correct. You also said she always wore slippers and would even go down the street to the shops with them on. That was so like my mum. You said that she had been sending me healing for high blood pressure and that she was glad that I had sorted it out. I must admit I had a wee scare but everything is okay now.

You also said "brother ", that my mum was with a brother. My mum and her brother had been separated when their mum died when my mum was only five years old. He went abroad and lived in Australia and Canada. He had traced my mum forty years later and she had gone on holiday to meet him and they had written back and forward but when I wrote to tell him that my mum had died I got no reply and I have written several times since and still no reply, so I had wondered if he too had died.

You also said that my mum was sending her love to my daughter, my brother and also James. James is my younger brother. My daughter was very close to my mum and you said that they were very similar in looks and in nature. That's true; my daughter misses her a lot.

I was so relieved my mum contacted me. As I said she has been in the spirit world for thirteen years and this is the first time she has made contact. In fact I was thinking that she was not speaking to me, that she wasn't pleased with me. The reason for that being that my mum was very ill and had to be put in a home before she died and everyday I would go and visit and every day she would look me straight in the eye and say "You put me in here. You better get me out!" I would go home in tears, but I knew she was in the best place for her where she could get the care that she needed.

A friend of mine who knew my mum was also at the demonstration you did and she came up to me afterwards and said how much she enjoyed listening to what my mum had to say and how it was so her – the way you described my mum.

I feel a huge weight has been lifted of my shoulders. The drawing looks like my mum but also like my daughter, who always wears scarves round her neck.

Yours sincerely, *Grace Forrest*.

Psychic Art - Case Study

Dear Marion,

My Reading - You told me you had my mum and described her and her character. She had Jim with her who was my uncle and also William, a little baby. That was my brother who only lived for two hours. My mother you said had a hearty laugh and you could hear her before you seen her. That was very true. You said that she was sending healing to me because I was suffering from stress and was not sleeping well, and that my Uncle Jim was saying " I am away for a walk ", and you felt he was suggesting I should walk and that it would help me to unwind and sleep better. My Uncle Jim did like to walk and always said he was away for a walk, no matter were he was going, especially if he was going to the pub for a wee while.

You also spoke of a quiet man that was with my mum and said you felt that he was my dad. That was also true. You also said my mum was with Nellie. The drawing is of my aunt Nellie, my mum's sister. I have sent a picture of my aunt Nellie.

I hope this benefits you with your book, *Rena Lennon*.

Psychic Art - Case Study

 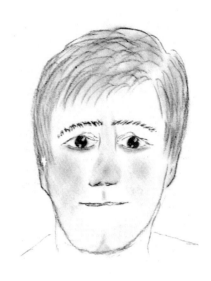

I had been asked to do a charity night in Elphinstone Bowling Club to help raise funds for the local primary and this is where Karen received her first experience of sprit communication.

This was the first time I had gone to a psychic evening and I did not know what to expect. I did not really believe in anything like that but I had gone along with my friend. Marion said she was aware of a young lad that had died suddenly and was about the age of 23. I did not think it was for me even though she was looking in my direction, but when she said his name was Derek then I knew it was my brother. Marion said he was sending love to myself, a wee girl and also someone called Donna. I was amazed because the wee girl is my daughter who Derek had never met and Donna was his first love.

Marion also said he was sending love and healing to my mum as she was having problems with acid in her stomach. My mum has an ulcer and had been complaining about it.

She also spoke about a grave that was like a football memorial but I was not too sure about that. She also mentioned that November was a significant month due to a ' passing' and that Derek was with this lady. Derek died in the month of November and so did my gran. When I got home that evening I was so excited I telephoned my mum who told me that the grave next to Derek's did have a football memorial and that Derek had been friends with that lad before he died. My mum when she saw the drawing was stunned at the true likeness to Derek. I do not have many photographs of Derek so it was so nice to get the drawing. I was on a high for weeks after getting the message and the drawing and it has certainly made me think, so thank you Marion and Frances. *Karen.*

Psychic Art - Case Study

Marion said that she wanted to speak to me as she knew that my mother was in the spirit world and described her as not very tall and having a small frame. My mum was less than five feet tall, with a very neat figure. Marion said my mother was worried about me because I was feeling exhausted and lacking in energy. This was true, I was feeling very stressed out by a few people at that time. My mother brought through two other ladies , a lady called Isa and my gran who Marion described 'as two peas in a pod'.

That is how my gran and her four daughters were known as 'peas in a pod ', because they were so alike. Isa was my mothers sister. They were concerned about a lady with the initial 'M'- that is my aunt Madge, Isa's twin sister. I did not know until a week later that my aunt Madge was due to go into hospital for a laser operation for a blood clot at the back of the eye.

'There is also concern regarding blood pressure with someone to the side of you '.My friend Cathy who was sitting next to me told me that she had just been told she was going to be having a short stay in the hospital to regulate this her blood pressure.

I was also told I would be taking a journey down the east coast. I had forgotten all about this but three weeks later I decided to go on a short holiday and that is were I went - Northumbria and Newcastle. The last thing Marion said was ' I need to mention the name of Annie '.

Both my gran and my mum are called Annie and the drawing is of my mum.

Thank you, *Mrs Anne Boak.*

Psychic Art - Case Study

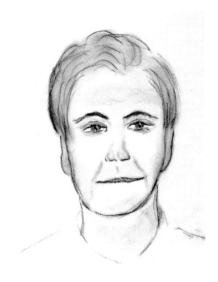

Dear Marion,

The key points of the message were as follows;

HUSBAND John - you said you were speaking to my husband whose name was John. YES.

CANCER TWO PLACES - My husband had cancer in his lungs which then spread to his head and ended up with two brain tumours as well. You indicated the tummy area at first which is where it could have started because the primary site was never known.

SHAVING - nursing staff had to do this for him and you said he hated being unable to do it himself. YES.

WORRIER - husband indicated I have become like this since he passed over. True there have been circumstances to cause this

GRASS - I have just changed part of the garden.

TWO SONS - my husband was sending his love to our two sons. YES.

IAN - you said healing was being sent to him. Ian is my brother in law and he has been attending hospital.

UNCLE WILLIE - YES, he is in the spirit world.

JOCK - YES, a friend of my husband.

STOMACH - Indigestion, wind swollen tummy. You indicated breast- bone area also and I have a hiatus hernia. You indicated medication was needed there as there seemed to be a gastric imbalance. YES.

BALANCE PROBLEM - I did have Menniers Disease which is an inner ear problem and needed two operations to correct it.

BLOOD PRESSURE - YES, I do have to watch it.

HIP, KNEE & LEG PAIN - YES.

You apologised for talking about all my ailments but that my husband was letting me know he was around me and wanted me to be well. That was typical of him.

You also said that I had been looking at photos and that I was thinking of enlarging one of my husband which I have since done. I enjoyed the demonstration you gave that evening, especially the drawing. The drawing is my husband John.

Thank you. *Joyce Scott.*

Psychic Art - Case Study

I have included this final drawing from Maria Hamilton but unfortunately, I do not have a suitable photograph.

My 95-year-old mother, Kathleen Fairney, passed away in January of this year, after falling and breaking her neck. I was grief stricken because the last five months of her life were so awful. In August, she fell and broke her hip and while being moved into a flat by herself after being in a care home for six years. She also broke her right wrist and was in terrible pain. She told me she was terrified of being on her own and so very lonely.

Five weeks after mum had passed away, I went to Marion's demonstration at the Glasgow Body and Soul Fair as Marion had brought through my dad four years previously when I was going through a very nasty divorce and what he told me was so encouraging and helpful. I knew it would be ok.

Two friends came with me, one who knew mum quite well. It was so amazing, we were crying and laughing.

Marion told me she was connecting with my mum who had recently gone to the spirit world and that she was saying," Did you see the state of my hair when I passed over."

.

Anyone who knew mum would know that is what she would say she always had her hair lovely. Marion said that although my mum was low in energy she was determined to come through because she was worried about me because I was not sleeping and that I should take Horlicks. She said she was with my dad and that they were looking after my family. My mum also had a message for my friend. She said that she had met her friend Lizzie who had passed over 6 months ago.

While Marion was talking, her mum Frances was doing psychic drawings and when she showed it to me I recognised it as my dad when he was younger.

It was all so wonderful and I got such peace knowing that mum was at peace and no longer suffering. My healing started there and then and I was able to pass it all on to my children to help them as they were also having trouble coping with the way she died.

My granddaughter Nicole who is only seven was going through a dreadful time because of bullying at school and had often talked about an older man who she dreamed of that was trying to help her. When I showed her the drawing, she said, "That's the man in my dreams". I am so glad that my dad is helping her.

I am so grateful to you both. God bless you. *Maria Hamilton.*

It never fails to amaze me when people from the spirit world bring forward information. Sometimes it is the simplest piece of information that has special meaning, e.g. on one drawing mum had drawn a wedding ring on a chain hanging round a gentleman's neck. The woman recognised the drawing as her father who was in the spirit world. He had been in a prisoner of war camp and whilst there had made the ring for her mother and had smuggled it out round his neck. She still had the ring, a token of love that was made in a time of hardship and separation. He, never knowing if they would ever meet again.

One young lad spoke about his trainers saying they were new; he had only worn them twice. For his heartbroken mum that was so meaningful. The trainers were bought for the gala in which his sister was the gala queen. He wore them that day, and three weeks later, he died tragically. His mum buried him in these trainers.

Sadly no amount of proof can be enough, nor can truly comfort a broken heart. The best proof has to be through individual experience, when you experience first hand the energy or essence of a loved one. If you have not had that proof, be patient you will receive it.

I often wonder if it was me in the spirit world trying to connect to my children what would I say that would be meaningful so that they would know it was me and no one else?

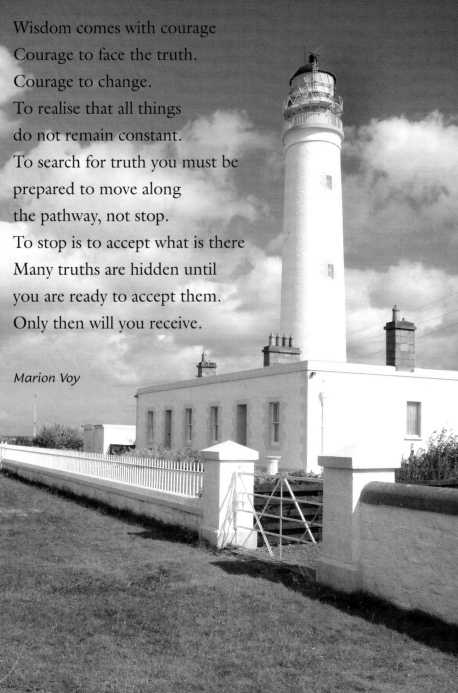

Wisdom comes with courage
Courage to face the truth.
Courage to change.
To realise that all things
do not remain constant.
To search for truth you must be
prepared to move along
the pathway, not stop.
To stop is to accept what is there
Many truths are hidden until
you are ready to accept them.
Only then will you receive.

Marion Voy

One quiet winters evening mum and I were at my friend Val's house and we decided that we would experiment with reading tealeaves. We were always experimenting with different 'tools' e.g. cards, ribbons, flowers and crystals.

We were exited as we went through the ritual of making the tea, drinking it, turning the cup upside down and turning it three times before looking deeply into the leaves. My mum went very still and I knew something was frightening her. She turned to me and said "Marion, I hope I am wrong but dad's going to die!' My heart stopped beating, I felt sick - she had to be wrong. Please God let her be wrong. Mum to this day will not read tealeaves, she says they are bad luck.

This was the first of many warnings we were given. In our meditating circle, we saw doves representing each of us, all were white except one, and it was black.

I am often asked if I am given information that is 'bad' and I tend to look at it not as bad, but that I am being prepared for what is to come so that I can face the situation with strength and that my mind and my emotions have time to prepare before the event so that I can deal with it in the best way not only for myself but for others.

Dad had been unwell and the doctor had sent him for tests for his heart but his heart was fine. Dad was later diagnosed with throat cancer, a diagnosis that came far too late. Within two weeks dad had undergone an operation to remove his voice box and the glands on the left hand side of his neck, which left him unable to speak, and having to breathe through a hole in his throat, which made eating extremely difficult. The day of the operation, I sat at his bedside waiting for him to 'come round '. As I looked at him, I knew he would never talk again. I would never hear him laugh as we discussed life and its greater meaning or listen to him singing off key, something we always laughed about. He would say that it didn't matter that his singing was so awful. What mattered was that he was singing from the heart and enjoying doing so!

It made me wonder, what was the lesson behind this illness? My dad was a quiet, kind man who was a dedicated healer? Why had this happened to him? Would life ever be the same? I could only imagine the fears that my dad had to face.

My dad was so grateful for the help he received from the staff at The City Hospital in Edinburgh and he wrote this poem to thank them and express how he felt.

YOUR WORLD

To all of you, whose lives touched mine.
You drew me into your world.
An added strength you gave to me.
The courage to face my adversity.

A stranger among you
With compassion you showered me.
Your caring overwhelming and unsurpassed.
Your patience hard to believe.

As I tried to communicate
With that which I had lost.
Your smile a gentle reassurance,
Gave me strength to try again.

With the tolerance of your care.
You sometimes understood
How best
My needs could be met.

Within your world, unseen
The gentle tears would flow
A silent cry for help was met
Within the caring of your soul.

Thank you for allowing me,
To enter into your world,
That mine could be a better place
All thanks to you and your loving grace.

W.R.Whaley

Dad came out of the hospital ten days later, walked right through the house into my back garden, started to wave his arms, and was pointing to the area that led from my wee sitting room. We gave him a pencil and paper and he drew an arch like seating area and proceeded to clear that area so that he could build what was in his mind. My husband Clive shrugged his shoulders and went to get the wood. Dad wanted to get on with life. To prove to us all he was fit and well. We all knew not to mollycoddle him, but let him deal with the illness in his own way. This area proved to be a tranquil quiet spot that attracted the birds and dad spent hours in the peace of what we called the wee sitting room looking out at the birds.

The family drew closer together to spend what time we had left. This was a period fraught with fear - yet hope, as we had to dig deep within ourselves to find inner strength and guidance. I don't know what was harder, the trauma of Ritchie dying suddenly or this process of watching dad die slowly. His quality of life becoming less and less each day so much so that I would lie in bed each morning frightened to get up in case dad had died in the night. I would lie and listen for the sound of him coughing so that I knew he was alive for another day.

The circle became not only a circle of wisdom but also of healing as we each got from the circle what we needed, but this did not stop the spread of the cancer to the right hand side of dad's neck. Dad had another operation to remove the glands and never really regained his strength. The cancer began to eat into his right shoulder resulting in an open wound which needed dressed daily. The doctor told us that it was only a matter of time before the cancer would eat through the main artery and this would cause dad to bleed to death. We took dad home and I was proud of how everyone dealt with the situation. Mum cleaning his wounds and easing his pain. My three children, Lynsey, Colin and Paul brought a quick energy of fun love and laughter into the house. Family and friends took the time to visit and give much needed encouragement and support.

On Saturday 11 May, there was a stillness in the house. My children were all out, mum and I were in the kitchen and dad and Clive were watching the F.A. cup final on the television. My dad loved football and wanted Manchester United to win. As the final whistle blew, my dad got up quickly and ran through to where mum and I were. He motioned to his shoulder which was bleeding heavily. We went through to the wee sitting room, sat dad down in his favourite chair and I held his hands and spoke quietly to him as the energy started to leave his body. He looked passed me to mum and said "Frances you are choking me!". He then fell into what looked like a deep sleep but he was dead, his soul had left his body. There was a sense of quiet and peace in the room yet mum and I were confused. Dad couldn't talk so how had he managed to talk and especially these words "Frances you are choking me". We were reminded of the past life experience in which he had choked my mum to death a lifetime ago, was there some kind of karmic debt taking place?

In our times of greatest need and pain if we look inwards and upwards , we find there is a strength and a peace we never knew existed and this allows us to connect with our true selves and to do what is right and to move forward instead of spiralling downwards into the depths of depression.

At that time the right thing for me to do was to take my fathers funeral. There was no way I was going to allow someone else to say these final words of what his life meant. In Scotland, you do not have to be a minister to take a funeral so I knew it was possible and it was what I needed to do for my own healing and as a token of love to my dad.

Mum was concerned, she thought that I would not be able to do it, that I would be too emotional on the day and it was unusual for someone other than a minister to take a funeral. However, I was determined to do it and my sisters Corrinne and Byrnice supported me in my decision.

So on the fifteenth of May I stood at the graveside, where I had first heard my nana's voice many years ago and spoke from the heart about the soul I knew as father...

My friend Beatrice said the opening prayer. Brian another friend read a passage from The Prophet by Kahlil Gibran on death. I read the words that my dad had spoken many years ago that I had taped at the time to try to prove to him that his philosophy was indeed inspired.

"While we are here on the material plain we do not see that which is hidden, the spiritual pathway of the soul.

I would like to talk of one who came - who was far above and beyond and had no need to come to the material plain but he came on a mission. A mission to show unto man that which is hidden. The pathway of the soul, the spiritual unfoldment of the soul.

If you look at the life of Jesus up until the baptisment, we see the trials, tribulations and the temptations. It is the pathway of every soul, no matter what colour the skin may be or whatever religion we may wish to follow. The pathway is the same, spiritual unfoldment - life itself.

After the baptisment, we see a great change take place. Perhaps we can see it best in the principle of the marriage ceremony where the groom waits at the alter and the bride comes in purity and so we see in the symbol of the ceremony spiritual reality taking place on the material plain. Also in the marriage ceremony, we see symbolised that which while we are on the material we must observe and work upon. We find that in the words "That which God has joined together let no man - no man put asunder."

Within these words, we find sanctuary of the individuality of the soul and in the teachings of Jesus, he shows us the way.

"Love yea one another."

"Love thy neighbour as thyself."

"Give unto others that which we demand for ourselves ".

The principle of the marriage ceremony is that which takes place in the spiritual world and that which we must adhere to."

We lowered his coffin into the ground to the music of Omm ne ma Shiva.

My children were not at the funeral, they were at school while the funeral was taking place. From the cemetery, you can actually see the school and that night my daughter Lynsey said, "Mum, I was looking over to where you were at the time of the funeral and I wished that I had said to you to let balloons off. That way I could have seen grandad's spirit floating up and up."

Balloons are what you associate with party and celebrations and I was reminded of her words of the band playing when Ritchie died. Once again, she was telling me that death should be a celebration from one world to the next.

If someone close to you dies, think about the funeral. What would be appropriate for the person who has died and for the family? If you do not have a strong religious background or belief, then think about having an alternative type of service. Organise music, poetry that has special memories and meaning. Ask family members to take part by reading a eulogy, playing an instrument. It may seem daunting to organise but it keeps you focused, involves the family and in some way it helps in the healing process.

No soul has ever connected with me to the same level as my dad. Never once did we have an argument or misunderstanding. Every moment of his company, I enjoyed and felt secure, contented, happy and loved. Would I be able to keep that alive now that he had gone into the spirit world?

55

I remembered that when I was a wee girl, I had always wanted a horse but there was no way that was going to happen and I would sit on his knee and he would tell me that when he died he would come back as a horse for me. He would show me the hair on his chest, all two of them, and say he was already starting to turn into one. As a child, I had never been afraid that he would die, yet now as an adult, I was afraid, afraid that I would loose that connection.

Never once did he ever say anything negative or critical towards me, nor I of him. It was like an in invisible barrier that was never crossed, because to cross it would violate a love that was unconditional.

I have tried to live to that standard with my own children, never belittling them or being negative in my deeds and actions towards them. Always supporting them even when they make mistakes because what are mistakes, other than lessons we need to learn. It is in the learning of these lessons we become who we are meant to be. I found that they too have never crossed that invisible barrier with me, even though I know I hurt them when I left their father years later.

My dad's death left a huge void that I felt could never be filled. Once again, I needed answers, I needed God. I needed to connect and gain strength from a higher power. Mum and I drew strength from our work in the churches and gave thanks for the many blessings we did have in our lives.

It was not long after dad died that mum came into the kitchen looking very confused," Marion do you think I have had a tragic life?"

"No! Do not be stupid, I think you have had a good life. Why?" I replied.

"It's just that when I was in the Co-op, a woman I'd not seen for years - said to me that it was nice to see me and that she often thought of me because I had had such a tragic life!"

Perhaps to someone else living mum's life and not having her strength and faith - then it would have been tragic, but as I have already said I believe it is from life's' hardest lessons that we learn the most and it is how we deal with these tragedies that make us who we are. It is through meditation that we can reach upwards and stay connected to the light and find inner strength, rather than let our energy spiral downwards and allow our energy to become de-pressed.

Some years later I was given an answer to one of my many questions when I least expected it. My friend Elspeth Walker teaches Reiki and because I had worked as a spiritual healer I was interested in receiving the reiki attunement. During the attunement I stepped back in time into another life and culture. I was a very young female with long dark hair, dressed in white robes and was walking along a pathway where people were lined on either side. I was taking part in some sort of sacred ceremony. I felt extremely spiritual and honoured to be climbing up a pathway of very steep steps toward the top where I could see a block of stone on which I was going to lie and be sacrificed to the gods. I felt extremely calm. The Marion part of me was analysing the situation and thinking " You idiot - you are going to be killed!!!"., but the part of me that was walking up the stairs believed in what she was doing and I became her as I calmly walked to the top of the stairs. I had been trained and prepared for this, it was my destiny. As I lay on the block I looked into the eyes of the priest who was going to perform the ceremony by cutting my throat - and I looked into the eyes of my dad filled with love ,pride and a hint of sorrow. I heard his voice in my head say "Marion - we have always worked together in many lifetimes. We always come to the material world together , then one has to work from the spirit side. In that lifetime , you went to the spirit world, in this lifetime it was my turn to work from that side. He held my hand as I bled to death. As I had spoke over his dead body at his funeral - he spoke over mine.

Once again a passed life connection had surfaced and once again there was a connection to the throat.

Within the memory of my soul
I remember you.
Your smile, your laugh
The essence that is you.
I would recognise you anywhere
Regardless of your guise.
It's in the eyes I recognise
The depth of who you are
And what you mean to me.

Marion Voy

PAST LIVES

Do you believe in past lives, that we have lived in a previous time?

This is a question that I am often asked, and the answer would have to be yes, I do. Mainly because I have had personal experience of recalling what I believe are past lives. I have found that recalling these memories have helped me to understand my relationship with those around me and helped me to understand myself. It has given me insight into why I react the way I do with certain people in my life and it has helped me to understand my fears. My past life memories with both my brother and my dad let me understand that I have lived with them in past lives , in this life and that there will be future lives to come.

When I found out that I was pregnant with my son Paul, I was shocked, even though my nana had told me, or warned me that I was pregnant. The doctor suggested I might want to consider a termination but I knew I badly wanted this child. I felt excited that he was going to be part of my life.

When Paul was born, I had this fear that I would loose him, that he would be taken away from me. This fear was very irrational. I had not felt like this with my two other children Lynsey and Colin, yet with Paul there was always this underlying fear. I knew that he felt it too.

Unlike Colin and Lynsey, Paul always slept in my bed, so much so that it was becoming a worry, as he got older. Not for me but for the family who would tease him that he was ' like a pimple on my ass!' Which was NOT true, he was not a mummy's boy – in fact he was and still is a bit on the wild side.

One night, mum and I were in the wee sitting room at the back of the house and I asked her if she would talk me back into past lives. I had been working with a new guide and I felt I knew him from another life and I wanted her to take me back so that I could have a look. However, she started to talk me back but not far enough back. What I was aware of was that I was this very small thin Jewish woman named Eva and I was standing at a train station somewhere in Germany. I was feeling physically sick with worry and fear. I was waiting for a train to come into the station and I was praying my son William would be on the train. At this point, I am aware that William is my son Paul in this life. I am also aware that if he were not on the train- he would have been caught and killed.

I look anxiously along the platform as people get off the train. Trying to see if I can spot him. Then the train starts to move away. Realisation dawns on me and I let out this deep moaning noise from the pit of my stomach, and the pain, the emotional pain was unbearable. Mum started to get frightened due to my distress and decided to quickly talk me back.

I have NEVER experienced pain like that in this lifetime, not even when my brother Ritchie was killed, and I hope I never do. The pain of losing your child is the hardest pain of all and this pain was real to me as I recalled this lifetime. I felt physically sick. I was shocked at the depth of pain I was feeling.

I now understand why I adore Paul so much and why I knew I needed to have this child. This also let me understand why I was so afraid he would die. It was not that it might happen. It was because it had. I had carried the memory of that intense pain from one lifetime to another. Was that the reason Paul was in my life? I never told Paul of this experience but from that night, he never slept in my bed again. It was almost as if the chord of fear had been understood, and therefore no longer existed between us.

I believe that our higher self / our spiritual self / super consciousness what ever label you choose to put on that aspect of our soul has stored within it; the memories of all the lives we have ever lived ,all the lessons and knowledge we have learned ,and knows the purpose of the life we have chosen to live now. That aspect of our self recognises people we have linked with in the past and in some way draws them towards us for many different reasons. How do we tap into that part of ourselves? Meditation is once again the answer, so start doing it!

Some years ago I qualified as a hypnotherapist and I have used this as a healing tool, particularly in the field of past life therapy. As I said earlier I can be quite analytical and like to question everything and so when Rosina asked me to do a past life session for her I asked her if she would mind if my mum came along and tuned in while I was doing the session. I was curious to see if mum would be able to tune into Rosina's higher self.

Rosina had come for regression because she felt that her life was not moving forward- that she was hitting a brick wall. She had done a lot of healing over the past seven years since the breakdown of her marriage and felt the time was right to move forward perhaps into a new relationship, but this did not seem to be happening. I was interested that the period was seven years. Very often things move in a seven-year cycle (seven-year itch) and therefore the seventh year is the death year, the ending or letting go to make room for the new. She was aware she needed to let something go but was not aware of what.

During the session, Rosina went back to a lifetime when she was a young girl. She was very sad because she had to leave her parents, her brothers and sisters to be married to an older man named Adam who lived in another village. She had no choice in the matter. Her father had arranged the marriage. She was very emphatic that she disliked the man and that he was hard and uncaring. We moved forward within that life to the birth of her son and then her death through some sort of illness in the lungs. When I asked her to look at the lifetime, a lifetime of sadness and misery that had been caused by the marriage to Adam. When asked what she had learned in that life she spat out the word OBEDIENCE.

Rosina was afraid to go into a relationship in case she had to be obedient and this would cause her to be sad and miserable. For the past seven years, she had led an independent life and she was afraid to jeopardize that, even although she did want a relationship. In the session, Rosina chose to recognise and let that fear go thus enabling her to hopefully now move forward. At the end of the session we asked mum what she had drawn. She showed Rosina a picture of a male that she instantly recognised as Adam and she quickly turned the picture face down – she did not want to look at him. The other drawing she liked, it was a picture of herself as the young girl in that life. Rosina took the drawings with her to reflect on, accept and to let go the fears she had, thus enabling her to feel confident that she could enter into a relationship and find the happiness and contentment that she was looking for and deserved.

Having been pleased with the results of this experiment, mum and I decided to look for a few other people to take part. This is how I met Hugh.

Hugh went into passed life energy very easily, and we were all pleased with the information that came forward. At the end of the session mum showed Hugh the drawing and said that at first she had thought she was drawing a guide but soon realised that this was a drawing of someone that Hugh had passed life memories with but that he actually knew him in this lifetime. She also felt that the person she had drawn was ill and that healing energy was being sent towards him.

Hugh recognised the drawing as his close friend Nick who was in India where he was involved in charity work. Hugh told us that Nick had been ill and that he had been sending thoughts out to him.

I asked Hugh if he would write something down regards the experience and this is the letter I was given.

I first met Nick when I was about eight years old and told him off for shouting at my dog. By the age of eleven, we were firm friends, and he even liked Shane, my dog and Shane liked him.

Nick was probably the first adult I had met who was actually interested in me as a person and was willing and able to teach me all or a lot of what he knew. In return for this, I swept floors etc, to earn my keep so to speak, much to his annoyance.

'Accept this as a gift little one, sharing this with you is payment enough' was often on his lips.

Just before my eighteenth birthday, I was at the dojo training (dojo is a martial art training school and Nick was the Dojin / master of the school) when I heard a noise and found Nick unconscious. He had some sort of fit and so I gave him resuscitation and it transpired that I had saved his life.

Just before my twenty-first birthday, I was passenger in a van coming back from a job one sunny November afternoon when I clearly heard Nicks voice telling me to bend down or get down on the floor NOW.

I woke up in hospital about ten days later with a mass of stitches in my face and was told that if I hadn't moved, the collision would have decapitated me.

There have been two other more minor occasions when we have saved each others lives although being miles apart. It's like we know when there's a problem or something wrong.

Nick has been my sense, my teacher and most importantly, friend for many happy years.

As I write this I've just heard from my friend. He is in India just now but has come to tell me to keep to the path of light and that he will see me in the next life.

I'm sorry for these tears but my friend has just begun the next stage in his journey twelve minutes past four U.K. time.

It is said from the dark cometh the light. A major light has gone out in my life but I know I will see him again.

Hugh.

Nick had passed into the spirit world as Hugh was writing this letter and reflecting on the bond between them, and their connection in this life. Mum had drawn the picture a few weeks earlier, a reminder that love knows no barriers of time, distance or realms. Hugh and Nick had linked in past lives, in this life and will no doubt link again in future lives. At the moment they still link together, Hugh in the material world whilst Nick still is his friend and teacher but from what we call the spirit world.

Within the wheel you are part of the whole.

Part of this world and the next.

Part of the future, the present and the past.

Part of each of your energy bodies.

In touch with the infinite, with all that there is.

Be still and all that is within - is inside you.

You are each breath of wind, each wave, each tiny insect.

Each soul that wanders the earth plane looking for the light.

Each soul that is enlightened and bringing to mankind

The knowledge and the wisdom of what is beyond.

You are part of all living thoughts

And have access to all realms

Be aware of the totality of you.

Marion Voy

When I started my spiritual journey over twenty years ago, it was difficult to find a spiritual teacher, so I started to meditate. To link with my own spiritual energy and I asked for guiding energy to come and help me on my journey. To answer my questions and help me to be a better person. To help me find what we all are ultimately looking for, inner peace, contentment and love.

I sat in two circles to help me to develop.

These guides or guardian angels I have come to love and trust and would advise anyone who wants to develop spiritually to dedicate time to link in this way.

It allows you to know yourself, trust yourself and to let go any fears you have. It builds within you a knowing that whatever happens in your life - you have the inner strength to deal with it and learn the lesson that is being taught, without fear. It allows you to remain within the light, rather than slip into the darkness of depression.

In the early circle that I had in my home, the purpose of that circle was that we each made a commitment to our own spiritual development and with that commitment, we took on personal responsibility. We were committed to ourselves, our guides and to each other. We met every Monday evening at eight o'clock and nothing would stop any of us from being there, our commitment was so strong.

I remember visiting my dad in hospital one Monday evening and though he was very ill and glad that I was with him he looked at his watch and said "Marion, you'll need to go or you'll be late for the circle", and I went. It was understood that my commitment was to the circle and the guides. I had made a sacred commitment to the guides to be of service and I respected that. I also knew that even though he was in hospital at eight o'clock he would close his eyes in meditation and 'tune in ' with us. If he could not be there physically, he would be there spiritually.

We called it a circle because for one we sat in a circle and because energy moves in a circular way, it is the law of nature. Bird's nests are circular as are spider's webs. Native American Indians call it the medicine wheel or stone circle, King Arthur and his followers sat at the round table. Stonehenge another ancient spiritual site is set in a circle.

We all took turns each week to open the circle in 'prayer'. The idea of the opening prayer is that when you close your eyes, you are closing out the material world and in that moment of stillness you are connecting with your heart and opening your heart to the spiritual world, to oneness. You are letting go the barriers you may have around your heart in the material world, barriers that we each place around the heart chakra to stop us from being hurt. To connect with your higher self you need to open your heart and give your love freely and unconditionally to yourself and to the other members of the circle. This creates an energy of love, light and trust that is needed for development. It is also an energy that is needed for the guides to easily come into the circle to communicate.

Then we would move round the circle, each person allowing his or her guide to come forward and to speak. By speak I mean words of wisdom, not psychic messages or messages from relatives in the spirit world. Before each person stood to speak, we would send our love and energy to that person by singing 'their hymn ', we each had our own hymn, a hymn we had chosen. Other cultures have used singing, chanting and drumming to create that same energy.

My dad's hymn was 'All Things Bright and Beautiful ', my hymn was 'By Cool Siloam's Shady Rill ' because it reminded me of Jack Winstanly, a man whom I greatly admired for his spiritual presence and teaching. Whilst your hymn was being sung you would close your eyes, go into the silence, take in the energy being given by the other circle members and use this energy to build and let your guides come in.

Once all the guides had spoken, we would discuss what had been said. We found that the guides on an evening would all speak on a particular theme but there would be slight differences in their opinions. We would stretch our minds to understand their philosophy, sometimes even disagreeing but it opened our minds and our hearts.

It also taught us to relax and allow spirit to come within our auric field knowing that the guides came in love. This was a great lesson for me for later on when spirit communicators would come into my auric field to pass on information to loved ones. I was and am still very comfortable with that and never afraid.

The circle taught each of us discipline, not only of commitment but discipline on what I call switching on and off to the spirit world, so that I was not picking up information twenty-four hours a day.

At the end of each circle we would close with prayer, the closing prayer allowing us to give thanks and to bring ourselves back to the material - to be grounded a term commonly used these days.

If you want to develop spiritually for your own development, as a healer, psychic or medium then I would advise you to start a circle with friends who are like-minded. Decide where you are going to hold the circle and when. Make sure you are holding the circle where it will not be disturbed e.g. by children refusing to go to bed and keep quiet, or by visitors continually coming to the door. This would stop you from being totally relaxed and going into the silence and would only cause frustration for everyone.

Decide when you are going to hold the circle e.g. every Monday evening at eight o'clock. Not five past eight but eight. In other words, everyone should be committed to each other and to the guides who are going to connect with you in the circle and you should attend every week. If you are tired, that should not be an excuse for non-attendance. How would you like it if your guides did not turn up for the circle because they were too tired?

I would advise you to each take turns each week of opening and closing the circle. It allows you to be confident in speaking in front of others, and creates equality within the circle.

In the first meeting of the circle you need to voice your commitment to each other and the guides so that you all know where you stand. You should meditate and know what you purpose is for being in the circle ? What are you seeking? What are your spiritual goals?

Having recognised that, then the second week you should be asking for guides or guardian angels to come in to the circle to help you.

I would also advise you to keep a personal journal of what you receive in the circle and how you are feeling. This will allow you to see how you are progressing and how you have changed when you look back on the journal later. Sometimes we worry that we are not making any progress but by reading the journal, you can see that you have come a long way.

How do I make a connection with my guide or guardian angel?

This is a question that I am often asked. You can make the connection in various ways.

1. Dreams – where there is a recurring dream of a guide. Very often this can be in a classroom situation where you are being taught or you are dreaming of reading a book.

2. In a meditation circle where you have asked for the guides to come in.

3. An experience when you desperately needed help and saw or felt a presence e.g. a near death experience or through praying for help.

4. An inner knowing.

5. Coincidence – where something is being shown to you repeatedly to make you take notice.

How do I know who they are?

Ask. Ask and you will receive.

SEEING - you may see a picture of a guide or guardian angel within your third eye.

HEAR - you may hear a voice. That voice may be very different from your own. You may hear the communication through your own thought waves but you will know the thoughts are not your own because the words and phrases used are very different from how you would normally speak and the philosophy given will certainly make you think and question its meaning. You may even just hear a name and know that is who is trying to help you.

SENSE - you may sense a presence within your auric field. By that I mean you will be able to sense wither the energy is male or female, young or old ,tall or short, large or small, serious or funny ,their culture or belief.

A signal or sign may be given to let you know when they are around e.g. tingling feeling or a tremendous sense of warmth and love.

In February of 1998, I developed a lump on my left breast and on seeing the doctor; he arranged for me to go to the Western General Hospital to have a mammogram. I decided not to tell anyone in the family for various reasons. One being that my dad had died with cancer two years previous and I did not want anyone to worry. If it was cancer, I wanted time to think it through because having seen my dad suffer with treatment to die anyway, I was not sure if I would want to be treated.

Secondly, my father in law, Les was in the Western General and nearing the end of his life. Les had severe breathing problems and was refusing to eat or drink. I did not want to add to the stress my husband Clive was already under. Therefore, I did what I do in times of stress; I meditated and asked for help and guidance.

Almost immediately, I was aware of the presence of a very small man who looked like a rabbi priest. He was very gentle and kind and said to me

"You have a worry regards your breast. This will be alright, the problem is two fold. The energy is not flowing freely into all areas of the breast and is causing a blockage. Physically you need to do vigorous exercise that will pump the blood quickly and with more strength round the body; emotionally you need to look at your relationship with your father-in- law.

This situation will help you to understand others and allow you to help them to heal themselves. Do not worry for self- there is a lot of good work to be done regards raising awareness of the spirit in others. You will spread your knowledge and your gift far. Be patient, be still ".

I immediately felt relieved that it was not cancer but it was cancer of a different sort, - an emotional cancer which is perhaps why it occurred in the breast - the heart chakra. I knew that I would need to take responsibility for what I had created in my own body.

My father-in-law and I did not have a good relationship. I disliked him and was very intolerant of him because he was an alcoholic. This dislike had built up over a number of years. The mammogram confirmed that the lump was not cancer but the doctor was unsure of what it was but told to me to come back if there was any change in it. I went into the hospital and spoke to Les and made my peace with him and came home and prayed for him from the heart. Les died, it was what he wanted, he was weary of living. Clive's family asked me if I would take his funeral. This was a further test for me. I had taken my dad's funeral out of love and I knew that to do this sacred task I would need to go even deeper within my own heart.

I stood over the coffin and spoke words of humour and love, reflecting on the man he was and I realised that he was a good man in his own way.

At the end of the funeral the undertaker asked if he could speak to me "I hope you don't mind me saying hen, but that's the best funeral service I've witnessed and I've witnessed a few and I just wondered ... If we have people who are looking for a service would you do it?"

I was shocked but said I would.

I even got orders from people who were there booking me to do their funeral when they died! Isn't life strange?

The lump disappeared a few days after the funeral and the wee rabbi guide that gave me his love and advice I have never seen again, but I know he's out there somewhere if I should ever need his help again.

I am often asked about guides and guardian angels and I always say –if you need help then ask them to come forward to help you. I was once asked how many guides are you allowed to have? The answer to that would be, as many as you ask for.

To let you understand I had worked with the same three guides for many years and whilst doing a course on crystal healing one of the tasks was to meditate in the directions of north, east, south, west, above, below and centre and ask for a guide to come - north ,east, south, west and centre in each direction ,WHAT?

That was going to be thirty-five guides. That was beyond my comprehension. It had taken me twelve years to build a relationship with three guides, what was I going to do with thirty five guides and why on earth would all these guides want to work with me or have the patience to put up with me! Plus the fact that I had made a commitment to these three guides. I did not have the time to give that sort of commitment to another thirty-five guides. I told mum what the task was and she just laughed "Marion, that's impossible ".

However, it was a task that I had to do and I thought 'What the hell… you have to try. Don't be so closed minded '. Therefore, I jokingly told mum I was going out to my workshop that morning to meditate for the first of the five guides, but if they had not showed face in the first half hour I was out of there!

Lo and behold, five guides and within half an hour, I was shocked to say the least. I couldn't believe it and neither could mum when I told her. So the next morning, I was going out to meditate for another five guides and she said " You're kidding me ,I'm going to come out with you and IF any guides come in I'll draw them. It has to be your imagination ". Okay, so out she came to my workshop. I sat on the floor with my notebook and pencil to write down the guides as they come in and to write down any information they gave. Mum was perched on the chair, paper and chalk at the ready.

We both closed our eyes and went into meditation mode. This is what I wrote down.

NORTH - Round faced, tanned, short bowl shaped jet-black hair - Mexican type? Simple man of the land, yet he understood the planets and their vibration for growing things on the land.

EAST - tall astronaut type - came to view the land - from the sun region - strong - leader - wise and ambitious. Sun god - blond with blond eyes!

SOUTH - young Egyptian, architect and builder philosopher and seer.

WEST - old Indian - *In my time I have seen many things - I have seen man turn against man for selfish reasons. We must understand that we are part of nature and to go against our rhythm brings disharmony.*

CENTRE - Buddha type person. *Be aware of your heart - live your life within your heart - not from the physical body, only from the heart and then you will become an enlightened soul. You will be balanced with all that there is - with the source. There will be no negativity no barriers or fears - no temptations of the physical realms. Live within the heart - be the heart - be unconditional love. You are then part of the source of all things. I come towards the earth to teach man to use the rhythm and vibration of the self, to return to the true self, the source - to the balance of all living things.*

I came out of the meditation paper in my hand thinking okay let me see what you have drawn!

NORTH   EAST

75

SOUTH

WEST

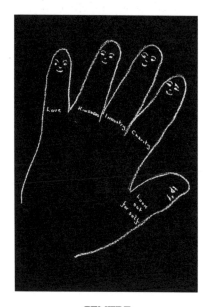

CENTRE

Drawing from the next morning

We were both a bit shocked when we compared what I had written and what she had drawn. Especially the sun god drawing. What were the odds of us both dreaming that up out of our imaginations?

I especially liked how she had drawn the Buddha image. The hand of friendship with small Buddha faces and the words, love, kindness, industry, charity and the thumb looking to the side with the advice to look out for self.

Was it my imagination, these guides? Were we so in tune she was able to link with my imagination? We were not sure what to think.

Next day we were both out in the workshop again and I am writing down the guides as they came forward. This time one of the guides was my dad who told me he was working with me, as I already knew but he wanted to join in on the exercise. I laughed to myself thinking 'I wonder how mum will feel drawing my dad ' However when we finished and were about to compare notes she said, "Before I let you see what I've drawn - one of the drawings is of a horse! I can't understand why?"

I laughed, my dad had always promised me when I was a child that he had come back as a horse and so he had kept his promised.

I found that I was not the only person that wondered if it was just a trick of the imagination or wishful thinking.

For years I had taught small workshops how to channel by linking in with their guides but even so they would doubt themselves and their own abilities. To overcome this I would often ask mum to come along to these workshops and 'tune in'. In other words, whilst I talked members of the group into meditation to link with their guides, she would sit quietly in the background and draw. Once out of the meditation, the group members would talk about their experience in the meditation and the guiding energy that they had encountered. Then mum would show them the drawing. They were amazed at how accurate the drawing was to what they were experiencing.

I have included three of these drawings, one an early black and white and another two more resent drawings.

I think it is good to always question and one person, Peter certainly did question himself that is until the guide that was talking through him started to talk in a foreign language, a language he was not familiar with. To satisfy his own curiosity he later taped the guide speaking though him and had the tape analysed. It was found that the language was an ancient Native American dialect.

This is a drawing of Roisins' guide and she was given these words of wisdom from the guide through a friend.

"On the banks of a river I sit and watch the water and I know in time you will come, and I will learn from you and you from me.

Many times our paths have crossed. I am a still person. I squat at the waters edge and I wait. Much can be learned from waiting and watching. Your tribe have lost their skill. You will re-learn. I think there is much you can learn from me in the silence. I sit and squat and I am still. My name is Norono , learn to be still. This is a good place to listen. I hear many things I do not think I want to know.

You are of your time and will know them. Be still and listen, as I listen to my forest."

This drawing was done for Brioney.

As Marion relaxed us, I was aware of spirits around me. She told us to ask guides to come in who would help us with what ever we needed at the moment. I remember asking for a guide to help me work with children, I work as a crèche assistant. As we went deeper and more relaxed, my first impression of a guide was a woman. She was young perhaps twenty five and she was wearing a dark perhaps black form of old style dress but on her head was a white linen style headdress which I took to be a nuns' headwear. It was starched and quite hard but flexible looking at the sides and seemed to be pinned up on top of her head. Rather like the nun in the 'Flying Nun' series, I had seen on the television as a child. Later the image changed to an older woman about forty five years old and her headdress came straight down either side of her face, more like a shroud but still in white. She told me her name was Frances and that she came from France. She had been pregnant as a young wife but unfortunately lost the child through a traumatic childbirth. She was unable to have more children and so abandoned she chose from there on to dedicate her life to working in a convent style setting caring for children. As she told me this, I felt an overwhelming wave of love and compassion for her. It made me feel truly emotional. I am pleased to have her help and assistance as I felt she truly loved children.

As a footnote, about 2 weeks later, I was with a couple of friends and we decided to visit the Gaughin exhibition at the National Gallery in Edinburgh. As I walked around and studied the paintings, I realised that my guide Frances could have come from that area of France. Gaughin painted many Breton women all dressed as I had pictured my guide. I was very drawn to the paintings of the Breton women; it was like a validation of the vision of my guide.

Briony Kelly.

This next drawing is a guide that was drawn for Rosina.

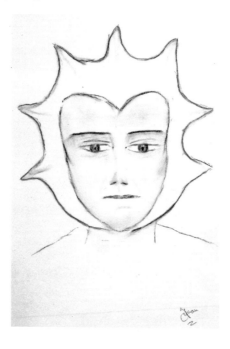

I had been doing Reiki on a young neighbour who is seriously ill and was at the time going through Radio and Chemotherapy. I had arranged for the girl to come back at a later date, but the girl's illness worsened. She had been on my mind before we went to Marion's to channel guides and also as we went into the meditation to link with guides and guardian angels.

During the meditation, I was aware of angelic energy which felt both gentle and at the same time quite powerful and carried the element of fire energy.

I was taken by the angels to a higher realm and given a very powerful crystal that was very heavy and very hot, which made me perspire a lot. My solar plexus area and my hands and feet were burning hot. I was told to work with emotional healing. I felt this healing angel was present to help me with healing the young girl. The angel's name was Heather and I now work with her on emotional issues.

Rosina

While working with Rosina, I was aware that the angel carried this message - *"If the emotions are healed then the body will heal, that is what I bring to you. Healing of the heart so that the children of this planet can mature and take responsibility, responsibility for themselves and their responsibility to others."*

The drawing as you can see is of an energy that looks nether male nor female yet has the fire energy around the head area and interestingly the shape of the face is heart shaped. The chakra of the emotions.

Is this all a figment of the imagination?

I only know, I take what is given to me in meditation with an open mind and ask that you do the same. I am not preaching to you or asking you to believe what I have experienced. I only know that for me it has brought me a sense of strength, peace and clarity in my life. It has answered many question but for every question answered it has led to even more questions. I have learned to ask the questions and to be patient and when I am ready the answer will be given but this leads to another question and another, a never ending spiral hopefully moving upwards towards enlightenment.

My daughter when she was young when asked what job I worked at would reply that I was a psycho instead of a psychic. Maybe there is some wisdom in that!

However, I know that I am not alone in my belief of guides and guardian angels. Over the years, I have taught groups of people how to link in with their own guides and angels and I know that they too have gained from that experience.

I am responsible for my every

Thought deed and action.

Therefore, I am responsible for

Who I am, what I am and where I am going.

For the past twelve years, I had been working as a medium and taking church services with mum, even running my own church in Tranent, carrying on the good work my friend Beatrice had started and all the while giving my services free of charge. It was what I believed in, and certainly, what my dad believed. You did not charge money for spiritual service to others.

However, I felt my guides wanted me to concentrate on my spiritual work, which was impossible because I also had a full time job, three children and a husband to take care of. The only solution would be to give up my job as a school meals supervisor and concentrate on readings and church work. However, I needed an income and the only way to achieve that was to charge for private sittings, for which I knew my dad would not be pleased. Therefore, the solution as usual in times of need - meditate. I did and brought forward my fears:

What if I could not earn enough money to cover my salary?

People that I mixed with in the church did not charge, what would they think of me?

If I was going to do readings, I wanted to work in a way that was different - I did not want to be another tarot reader even though I love my tarot cards. In the past I had always worked with spirit communication for people who were bereaved and I was beginning to realise that people needed help and guidance with other traumas in their lives e.g. divorce, illness, job, children, relationships. I wanted to work on a psychic level as well as a spiritual level. I knew that if I put my questions forward they would be answered, maybe not immediately and in the way I expected but I knew to trust and be patient.

I had worked as a school meals supervisor for Lothian Region for sixteen years and loved my job and the women I worked with but due to 'government cutbacks 'they decided to offer voluntary redundancy to staff at my level. A few days later I was sitting at my desk when I opened a letter informing me I had x amount of years and days until I retired at sixty-five. I had a vision of my dad and the realisation that he had worked hard all his life and never lived long enough to retire. I picked up the phone, called head office and asked them to send me the paperwork. I left three months later, a huge leap of faith. I was sure that the money I received though small would be enough to see me through the first year of business - so I knew the risk was less. I had a cushion to fall back on.

I was talking to a friend about my apprehension regards charging for readings as it went against what I had been taught and she astonished me by saying, "Marion, you gave me a sitting two years ago which helped me a great deal and there have often been times I would have loved to ask you for a sitting but I know how busy you are and that you would not take anything for the reading, so I did not like to ask".

That made me think, was I denying help to people by not charging? People who could not afford a reading would still get a message in the church. Maybe I needed to change my way of thinking, I know if I need a haircut I need to pay the hairdresser for her time, skill, and I certainly do not grudge the money because it makes me feel so much better. Still it caused me pain - What would my dad think? I decided that he had supported me all my life so of course he would support me in this.

Therefore, I started my own business as it was, not too certain of what I was doing, but knowing that this was what I loved and the work gave me so much satisfaction. I was not sure how to market what I was doing; I still needed something different, a way to work that was unique. Again, I meditated on it - but it was not being made too clear to me, all I could see was an array of colours.

I decided to do health and healing fairs and take my tarot to do readings. Mum thought we should have something else on the stall to attract people across. She had seen something in a craft magazine called encaustic art, thought we should send for it, and see what it was. It was coloured wax that you melted on a small iron and put on card to form pictures. The pictures were beautiful, so we thought we could make cards at the stall.

The first fair we did, I was very nervous, it was all new and I was going to be charging for my work, for a tarot reading. We got to Meadowbank Stadium in Edinburgh where the fair was being held, only to discover that I had forgotten my tarot cards. I could not believe I had left them at home! I am normally very organised and it was not as if I had a lot to remember! That meant we had paid for a stall and could not do readings. I telephoned Clive to look for my cards and bring them in. In the mean time we had a table with coloured wax and an iron. A gentleman from the National Federation of Healers came forward and asked mum what we were doing.

" Pick me three colours and I'll make you a card", said mum. He chose his three colours, she melted them together put them on the card to form a picture, and then she looked at the picture and proceeded to tell him things about his life. A young girl then came across, and asked me what we were doing, "Pick me three colours "and I followed mums lead and read the card, the same way you would read tea leaves or a crystal ball, telling her about her life- past, present and future. So the final part of the jigsaw was made known to me through my mum.

We had a way to work that was different and that linked on all levels, spirit and psychic. On the card, you were able to see spirit faces, read initials, see various symbols and the nice thing about it was the client was able to see it too, and once the reading had taken place the piece of card we placed in a card frame for them to keep as a reminder of the reading.

This has become our trademark as no one else reads in this way. I call the cards Chakra Cards because the colours link in with the auric field of the person relaying what is going on within them on all levels, physical, emotional, mental and spiritual. Over the years, we have been amazed at what has come forward on the cards and how meaningful they are to the sitter. None, more so than the card I made for myself, which is the front cover of this book.

Mum and I attend the Body and Soul Health and Healing fairs run by 'the two Donald's', Donald Busby and Donald McKinney. Whilst at one of the fairs in the Concert Hall in Glasgow, my energy was low and although it was only half-past four, I had decided that I was not doing any more readings.

A woman came up to our stand and asked what we were doing. I told her about the wax and that you had to choose three colours. The woman was being obnoxious towards me and obviously did not believe in spirit or in psychic energy. I think, she thought it was a con.

I am not out to try to covert people to my way of thinking. Like the Gnostics, I believe we need to, and can find the truth within ourselves through our own personal experience. I will tell you of my experiences in the hope that it will encourage you to seek out what you need for your own growth. I am the first to admit 'I do not have all the answers '.

I was annoyed, but was not going to show her how I felt. Dad always taught me to be patient. So I took a deep breath and calmly said, "If I was going to make a card for myself, these are the colours I would choose ", and I proceeded to make a card for myself. When I looked at the card I was amazed at what I saw. At that time, my husband and I had just separated. The family home had been sold and I had just moved into my wee house in Macmerry, which was to become a safe haven for me, a new start, a new beginning, the light at the end of the tunnel. However, there was a dark cloud hanging over me. There was so much emotional trauma not only for myself, but also for Clive and our three children, which we were trying to work through. This was all reflected in the card.

When I looked in the bottom right-hand corner - there was my dad! My dad had fuzzy hair, a beard and a big nose. You can see the energy gathered above the throat representing the throat cancer but what was most astonishing was the red that was flowing from the right shoulder representing how he had bled to death. I felt this was my dad giving me approval for the work I was doing, for charging for sittings and once again letting me know he was working with me and supporting me in the changes that were going on in my life. I decided to use this picture on my business card, to remind me that he is always there, only a thought away.

The other part of the card that interested me was the snow goose in the future (I always read the card from the bottom up past, present, future) representing a visit to Canada, and I thought 'there's no way that I was going to Canada. I was already planning to go to America to visit my daughter Lynsey, which I was a bit apprehensive about as I was travelling on my own and I had not done a great deal of travelling.

When I did travel in the May to visit Lynsey I arrived in Amsterdam to get my connecting flight only to be told that they had overbooked the flight and I could not get on the flight! I was so angry, how can you overbook a flight. The company know how many seats are on the plane and anyway I had my seat number! However, they had and I had to fly to Canada to get a connection to America. When we got to Ottawa, the runway was frozen and the plane could not land. This resulted in us flying to Montreal where we landed, refuelled and flew back to Ottawa, by which time I had missed my connection and had to stay in Canada overnight. To make matters worse I had no contact number for my daughter to inform her where I was! I remembered the picture and was not sure if the snow goose was a warning or dad letting me know that it would all be okay. I did eventually arrive in Boston the next day.

I love working with the wax. The picture that is created is a reflection of that person's life. It fascinates me how the colour and imagery can be interpreted so accurately. I have included a few examples so you can see how it works.

Psychic art of a different sort.

Ultimately, I believe we create the picture of our lives, and the colour within our lives by our thoughts, deeds and actions, past and present which affects the future. Which is why I believe that we are each responsible for our every thought deed and action and are therefore responsible for who we are, what we are and where we are going.

I have included two examples of chakra cards and the story that each card told. It is my dream to write a book on this subject so that others can enjoy working in this way.

Chakra Cards - Case Study

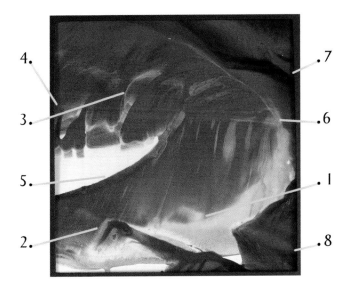

1. The first thing I am drawn to in your picture is the blue shape of a male face and he is showing me that he was in a hospital bed before he died. The light blue tells me he is a gentle, quiet spoken man and the fact that he is central in your card means he was central in your life, so I feel that this gentleman is your dad. He is drawing my attention to the figure in white and as he, left his body this lady was waiting for him in the spirit world. I feel that this is his mother.

"Yes, my dad was a quiet man and he died just over a year ago and he did mention his mum before he died."

2. The sharp red tells me this was a sudden unexpected passing. He is giving me the name of William and this gentleman is also in the spirit world with your dad.

"Yes my dad did die suddenly, and William is my father-in-law."

3. He is showing me a skull on the card and I feel that this is connected to how your dad died.

"My dad had an aneurysm in his brain."

4. The dinosaurs indicate that he was very set in his ways e.g. he always wore a hat.

"That's true."

5. This long area is thread, and for some reason I want to connect your dad to sewing.

"My dad made his own flies for fishing and also worked as a cobbler and used a sewing machine."

6. I feel I am seeing A or the month of August.

"My birthday is in August."

And I also feel he is sending his love to a wee boy that links to you and someone whose initial is A.

"The A is my sister and the wee boy is my son."

7. He is also showing me a new branch on a tree.

"That could be the family tree; his first great-grandchild is due to be born."

8. He is showing me this area as a sad area in his life. I feel it is regret that he never got to say "goodbye" to someone that was close to him before they died and he felt guilty about it.

"His brother died and he was not told his brother was ill until after he died, and he was very angry about that."

9. He is speaking about "the picture". There must be a picture that is significant to him.

"Oh, that's funny. He had bought this picture, which has been under the bed, and last week my mum took it from under the bed and hung it up"

I know that you want me to change your name for putting this in the book, so if it is all right with you can I put your name in as Ann.

"Yes, that was my grandmothers name. Thank you."

Chakra Cards - Case Study

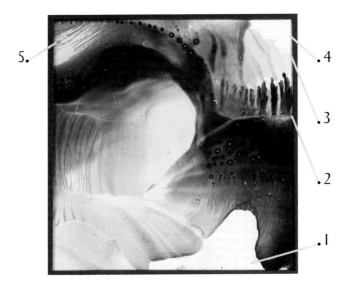

This was the first card that Marion had made for me and the only detail she had was my first name, Moira, so the reading was surprisingly accurate.

1. The reading began with the "missing" figure in my life that Marion identified as my mother who had died five years ago. What was interesting was that I had come to see Marion because I felt my mother was urging me to do so, that she had something that she wanted to tell me. Marion said that there was a link to America, did I have a brother over there? That there was unfinished business.

I was shocked, because my mother had been married to a Joe Bragg and had stayed in the New England area, where Joseph worked for the family construction business. He was killed in an accident when a lift cable severed resulting in the lift plummeting to the ground. My aunt remembers my mum being heavily pregnant at this time but on her return to Scotland, my mum could not recall what had happened, and later she married my dad. I have always felt that I have an older brother and I think perhaps mum wants me to track him down.

2. Marion moved on to another part of the card that she described as a bridge, and on the bridge there were standing small children and politicians that were being consulted.

3. The yellow energy flowing under the bridge was learning or education.

4. The white energy above their heads was my goal, something that I was aiming for but that there was a huge barrier and doubts stopping me achieving this. The barrier was the dark blue area with the dots, the dots representing the doubts.

The other reason I wanted to consult Marion was because for the past twelve years I had been struggling with financial problems connected to a small children's nursery and was in fact meeting with councillors and politicians the next week in an attempt to save the nursery from closure. Marion's reading picked up on all this and the bridge was appropriate because the nursery was called Bridge Street Nursery.

5. Marion then spoke of the white area in the top left of the picture and said that my mum wanted to let me know that she was with someone called Alexander, and then she laughed and said, "We call him Sandy." This related to a dream my daughter had previously where her grandparents were in our garden and had with them a boy aged about twelve. The boy was the same age as my youngest son, but my daughter had no idea who he was. In the dream, my mum told her that she and my dad looked after this boy.

Within weeks of my youngest son being born, a close cousin lost a baby boy and we had spent time together at the hospital afterwards .The baby she lost was very like my son Danny and I have always felt a sadness for his short life. The boy's name was Alexander and how like my parents to shorten it to Sandy.

Lastly, Marion spoke of my mother again and this was so ironic and really for me was conformation as to the character of my mother. Marion was a bit embarrassed to say that I was to look at my tealeaves "you know you can" and then look deeply at myself .No one could know of this detail in my early life. The old Scots tradition of reading tea leaves and how my mother would tell me not to look at my own cup and then she would be drawn into reading my cup by me saying "but mum look at that."

QUESTIONS ?

How long does it take before someone will make contact?

When someone dies they try to make contact right away, to bring reassurance to those left behind that they live on, in the spirit world. I find that within the first few weeks there is very often a lot of what I call electrical activity e.g. kettles, televisions, music centres being switched on or off, lights having a surge of electricity. This is especially the case when there has been a sudden death. The family are in shock and that energy can be used to create psychic phenomena, whereas when there has been a long illness before the passing the energy around the family can be different. Very often, there are dreams and visions in which the person will appear trying to bring reassurance to those left behind.

The length of time before contact is made can also depend on the determination and character of the person who has died.

Many years ago, mum and I were working in a church in Armadale and the very first message was for a young man named Willie who was seated at the very back of the church. The woman in the spirit world was a wee very old woman who gave her name as Margaret and said she was his grandmother. She was a very strong bossy character and gave a list of names of people she was with including her son, who was also called William and had died some time ago. She then proceeded to lecture him about what he was doing with his life and what he should be doing. She was very opinionated, and I jokingly reminded him that just because the advice was from spirit it was not from God, so he should make up his own mind. At which point I felt a sharp pain in my side and I knew that she jabbed me in the side with a knitting needle to let me know to mind my own business and keep my opinion to myself! The drawing was of this wee wizened old woman with a real spark in her eyes.

Afterwards Willie came up and said, " Marion, I knew she would come through tonight, that's why I came along. We got a phone call from the hospital at ten o'clock this morning to say we should come in as she was dying. I could hear her voice in the background shouting, Tell them not to hurry, I've ordered my lunch and I'm going NOWHERE till I've had it!". She died at two o'clock this afternoon."

Another occasion was a demonstration I gave at The Fireman's Club in Leith a few weeks ago. A woman came forward to speak to her daughter and spoke about The Infirmary and that she had died there. She said that she would have preferred to have died at home but it did not matter. That she had died before her family had a chance to get there, but it did not matter. What mattered was the love that they had shared and she did not want them to feel regret because they were not there at the time she passed. She mentioned that she had heart problems that although not serious, a problem involving fluid had occurred and because of this, she had died quickly. She gave names of people that she was with in the spirit world and mentioned that she would always be there for her granddaughter as a guardian angel to watch over her.

She also mentioned that she had tried to contact them by switching off a light.

After the demonstration, I went over to speak to the woman, as I could see from her reaction that she was shocked.

"Marion, I cannot believe that happened and what you have told us. My mum died this morning unexpectedly and we never got a chance to get into the hospital in time. The funny thing is that my brother was on his way in to the hospital, while my sister-in-law stayed at home. At 3.45am, one of the lights blew and she could smell the distinctive smell of the hospital and sensed something had happened. My mum died at 3.50.am.

I work here at the club and I never told anyone what had happened, I wanted to see if by some miracle she would try to make contact with us.

Although her passing is a shock, I feel so glad that she has come through. I feel a deep sense of peace instead of sadness. So thank you."

I felt so glad that Maureen's mother had made contact and brought forward not only where and how she had died but also that she had said that it did not matter, that they were not there at the time. I see so many people that feel guilty that they were not there when the person passed. The funny thing is, if they had known they would have been there. Yet they carry that feeling of guilt or disappointment like a burden and beat themselves up with it repeatedly.

I am also aware that because the family were not at the hospital, she went to see them before or as she passed. Therefore, if you cannot be with them perhaps because you are in their thoughts then they come to you, to say goodbye.

Countless people have had experience of this as a vision, or just a feeling of sadness and a knowing. If you did not get the chance to say goodbye or do not get the chance, then take the time to go to a favourite quiet spot and say goodbye in your own way. Please do not carry that pain with you, it serves no purpose.

Do you ever get anything 'bad' for yourself?

I wouldn't use the word' bad ' but I do get what I call warnings of things that are going to happen, and I think these warnings are so that I can prepare myself and therefore react in the best way in that situation.

When my son had just turned sixteen he brought home this wee girl Lesley that he was going out with. Immediately I felt very protective towards her. She was tiny compared to my son who is over six foot tall. I could hear the word 'Pregnancy 'repeatedly in my head.

After she had gone home I took him aside and gave him the 'condom lecture ' better to be safe than sorry and I said that if he could not afford them then I would buy them for him! He was mad with me and informed me rather loudly, "They were not doing anything" In other words - mind your own business. However this warning persisted, so I few months later I asked him if she was pregnant. "Don't be stupid!" was his reply.

Then I had a dream in which I saw a wee baby boy and when I asked I was told his name was Lewis and he was due on the 22nd April, my son's birthday. Once again, I asked Colin if Lesley was pregnant and again he said no. By now, I was beginning to think that I was going nuts.

When he did eventually tell me in December, my first feeling was relief that I was not going off my head and I did not react angrily. I had had months to think about what I would do in that situation. I was able to say that I would do all I could to support them both. This resulted in us all remaining calm and not creating a drama in an already traumatic situation. So much so, that Lesley asked if I would like to be present at the birth of 'our wee Lewis '.

That day was filled with so much emotion as I watched this wee life being born and my son going from being a boy to a man in that moment. I was so proud of how both he and Lesley handled the situation and I still am.

However, had I handled the initial situation differently then I am sure my relationship with Lesley would have been very different and she would not have asked me to be at the birth and share that very intimate and special time with them.

Do you ever have any spirits come through that the person might not want to be in contact with?

That tends not to happen, although whilst working in Dundee I had a message from a young lad in the spirit world that connected with another young lad in the audience. The lad in the spirit world gave his name, and spoke about cards and described the tattoos he had and mentioned the fact that he had been stabbed, and that this was the cause of his death. I could see the young lad in the audience was getting paler and paler as the message went on.

He came to talk to me afterwards *"That was scary - it was me that stabbed him! He thought I had been cheating at cards and he waited for me coming out the pub and stabbed me in the back. I stabbed him back in his chest. It wasn't my fault. I did time for it! "*

Do people that commit suicide go somewhere else ?

Are they punished for taking their own life?

I was once asked to take a funeral of a man who had taken his own life and as I prepared for what I was going to say at the funeral my mind kept going over the question of suicide. Are people punished for taking their own life or is it the case that they punish themselves when they see the grief that has been left behind. I heard a voice say

"Marion you believe that we each choose to come to this earth plane, because we have free will. Then you will also understand that we have free will should we choose to leave it ". I have pondered over these words many times.

I do know that I have communicated with many people in the spirit world who have taken their own lives and they are no different from other spirits in that they are concerned with the health and wellbeing of their family and want their love sent to them.

Have you had to go anywhere that was haunted?

Sometime ago my friend Beatrice was asked to go to a house in Kirkcaldy that was haunted and asked if mum and I wanted to go along with her. By haunted I mean that there was a lot of psychic activity; the television was being switched on and off, curtains being pulled down, objects being moved etc. The young lad who was living in the flat was terrified, as was his friend who was often in the house.

Beatrice was aware of an old man in the spirit world who had lived in the house previously. He was angry that this lad was in his house watching his television and each time he asked the young lad and his friend to get out, they ignored him! He wanted more coal put on the fire because he was freezing and he wanted to know where Betty was and why had she not she been in to see him.

I asked him if he could see the golden light in the corner of the room but he said "no". He did not seem to realise that he had died. I could see small plump woman with dark hair and rosy cheeks standing behind him. She told me that when she was alive she " kept him right " but after she died he had let himself go. He was not eating properly was drinking too much and had been very depressed. I knew that she had to be his wife. I asked him to close his eyes and to think of his wife. "She's dead, hen" he replied. As I looked at her she started to rub his neck and shoulders. I asked him if he could feel anyone rubbing his neck. He said he could and when I asked him who was rubbing his neck he was silent for a moment and then replied with disbelief

"My wife.

Am I dead?

I thought I'd had too much to drink.

I'm sorry hen.

Thanks for helping me ".

At which point he turned towards his wife, smiled, and went with her.

The lads were relieved that the problem had been dealt with, but as we prepared to leave, we were aware of a woman in the spirit world. It was the mum of one of the two lads. She desperately needed to contact her son to say to him that she wanted him to get on with his life and enjoy himself. The lad was very emotional. He told us that he and his mum were very close and that she had died from cancer. While she was in hospital, he had promised her that he would never leave her and that he had put a letter in her coffin saying that he was going to take his own life and would join her shortly. He confessed that he had not managed to pluck up the courage to commit suicide, but that he thought about it every night. While we were there my mum had been drawing and had drawn a portrait of his mum, which he recognised. He was delighted , his face beamed and he could not stop smiling.

I felt so sad that this lad missed his mum, but we were able to convince him that his mum did NOT want him to join her in the spirit world. He was so relieved, it was like a weight had been lifted from his shoulders.

The psychic activity stopped but I am not sure if it was the old man that was causing it, or the young lads mum. They both wanted to be noticed but for different reasons.

Do we have a time here on earth and when our time is up, we die?

I am often asked this - especially when someone young has died in tragic circumstances?

I must admit I too asked this question when my brother died.

That question plagued me - why him, why so young when he had everything to live for?

I was looking through photographs taken the Christmas before he died. Photographs portraying a happy time. There was only one photograph of Ritchie and in that photograph, you can see the clock in the lounge. The clock is showing the exact time he died.

Another weird thing, was that the week before he died he had got out all his photographs and put them together in a scrap book, a reflection of his life. My mum had also felt that he was acting strange and she had a feeling that he had something to tell her. Was he aware on a super-conscious level of the events that were to follow?

Final Words

This book is my story and also my mum's. Neither of us were born mediums. We each have strived in our own personal quest to find out if there is life after death, if there is a spirit world.

I questioned everything and still do and if I were to give advice to you it would be…

First you need to know what you want in your life. There is no fair wind to take him who does not know where he is going.

Secondly "Ask and you will receive ". I have asked for many things and asked many questions. I have nearly always been given what I have asked for. Maybe not in the way I expected or when I wanted it, sometimes I have had to wait years, perhaps because I was not ready to accept the answer or I had to wait until the time was right.

Look for and try to understand the lessons you are learning and take that wisdom with you as you move forward in your life's journey. A journey that is special and unique for each of us.

Lastly, live your life from the heart, have good intentions and when things get difficult think on these words -

I am responsible for my every thought, deed and action.
Therefore I am responsible for who I am,
what I am and where I am going.

Enjoy the journey and *remember* that you have the power within to create that which you desire.

Marion Voy

THANKS

I thank both my parents for the part that they have played in my life but most of all, my thanks go to my brother Ritchie, whose death changed the direction of my life and gave it meaning.

RITCHIE WILLIAM WHALEY

Son, brother, boyfriend and biker.

You are to us, all of these.

Your lopsided grin and lazy stance

Your love of life, no fear of death

And when that moment of death occurred

You left without a second word.

We miss your body, yet know your soul.

We feel your presence when you are near.

You give us your love the strength to go on.

You know no death, your life goes on.

You've proved to us to have no fear.

That life is eternal, God's golden rule.

There is life, there is no death.

To purchase this book, for information on talks and workshops given by Marion Voy and for demonstrations by both Frances Whaley and Marion

Visit www.marionvoy.com

Marions next book - Chakra Cards - The beginners guide will be available from June 2006.